Legacy of George Fernandes

The Institute of Social Sciences was founded in 1985 to study contemporary social, political and economic issues and problems in an inter-disciplinary perspective and to make available its findings and recommendations to government bodies, social scientists, policy makers, people's and workers' organizations, so as to widen their options for action. The evolution of an informed and action-oriented public opinion is the primary aim of the Institute.

The research projects undertaken by the Institute cover a wide range of subjects in the areas of decentralization and local governance, women's studies, democracy, human rights, environment and contemporary economic and political issues. The Institute also organizes seminars, workshops, discussions and training programmes for the exchange of ideas and dissemination of its research findings.

The Institute seeks to build a community of concerned scholars and activists for ushering in a humane and just society.

Institute of Social Sciences
8 Nelson Mandela Road, New Delhi 110 070, India
Phone: 91-11-43158800, 43158801, Fax: 91-11-43158850
Email: issnd@issin.org; www.issin.org

Legacy of George Fernandes

Edited by
George Mathew

AAKAR

Legacy of George Fernandes
Edited by George Mathew

First Published 2020

ISBN 978-93-5002-657-1

Published by
AAKAR BOOKS
28 E Pocket IV, Mayur Vihar Phase I
Delhi 110 091, India
www.aakarbooks.com

In Association with
Institute of Social Sciences
8 Nelson Mandela Road
New Delhi 110 070, India

Layout and Design: P. Nandakumar

Cover Photo sketch by: Sitt Nyein Aye (Mandalay, Burma)

Laser Typeset at
Arpit Printographers, Delhi

Printed at
Sapra Brothers, Noida

Foreword

This volume, *Legacy of George Fernandes*, with contributions from George's close associates, friends and admirers, is a modest effort to remember George and his political life and legacy. He fought for the rights of the working class and the underdog and remained political colossus on the national scene for several decades.

The first time I met George Fernandes was in Bangalore in Pattabhi Rama Reddy's residence along with Snehalata Reddy in 1972. Here was a man of the masses who was cut out for a bigger role in national affairs!

Since the mid-seventies, when I was a Research Scholar at the Centre for the Study of Social Systems of Jawaharlal Nehru University, New Delhi, doing my Ph.D. on a much complex theme of "Communal Road to a Secular Kerala", George Fernandes remained my inspiration and a great source of strength. Then George Fernandes was well known as a militant socialist who was too impatient to stick to a political party; a leader who made the trade union an effective weapon of political struggle; a revolutionary who took to underground resistance in fighting the Emergency; and a giant-killer and a 'fighting loser' at the hustings. He was an inborn trade unionist, an unfailing friend of the working class, a human rights activist with an international perspective, and a unique politician who dared to be in the eye of almost every storm. When I was at the Jawaharlal Nehru University George Fernandes was leading the workers in Kolar Gold Field, etc., which gave George a fame and won him a large number of followers. I wrote about that struggle.

During the anti-Sikh riots of November 1984, George took the lead in constituting the People's Relief Committee with Justice Hidayatullah as Chairman. By November 6, there were more than 60,000 refugees in various camps in Delhi alone. As a member of the People's Relief Committee, I was also a member of the fact-finding committee along with S.K. Goyal, Sudhindra Bhadoria, Javed Habib and Yashwant Sinha.

After struggling for more than six months with the idea of establishing a centre in Delhi, where intellectuals, researchers and activists could study contemporary social, political and economic issues and problems, I went to George with a concept note. He extended unstinting support. I would like to acknowledge here that without George's support and patronage—ideological, financial and in terms of networking—the idea would not have found institutional expression.

I still remember the first Governing Body meeting of the Institute of Social Sciences on 2 September 1985 in the board room of the New India Cooperative Bank at P. D'Mello Road in Mumbai. Besides Professor D.T. Lakdawala, Chairman, the following members were present in that meeting: Shri T.S. Kannan (Vice-Chairman), Professor Aloo Dastur, Shri Vijay Tendulkar, Mrs Jaya Jaitly, Mr Sudhindra Bhadoria. George was with us throughout in the meeting. Since then in the several Governing Body meetings that followed as well as in major academic activities, George remained with us. As far as the Institute of Social Sciences is concerned, George Fernandes was a friend, philosopher and guide.

Political issues are seldom linked with such harsh and intense reality to the life of an individual as in the case of George Fernandes. For over four decades, he was in the thick of the political struggle in India, challenging the corrupt, oppressive and dehumanized system with reckless courage. In his fight for the poor and the oppressed, he spoke and wrote with fervour and realism unmatched in contemporary times.

Apart from his unflinching faith in the efficacy of democratic socialism for resolving India's socio-economic problems and achieving the upliftment of the poor and the indigent, George Fernandes developed a deep interest in the growth of international socialism. He gave it a new dimension and orientation keeping in view the needs of the people in the Third World countries. He did not fight shy of taking up cudgels against his European counterparts whenever he felt their approach did not adequately reflect the hopes and aspirations of the people in the developing countries.

George Fernandes made history of sorts by being in and out of prison no less than fifty times in post-Independence India for periods ranging from a week to a year. During most of these imprisonments, he was denied such common amenities as books and periodicals and was, more often than not, treated as a 'C' class prisoner.

His demise on 29 January 2019 was an irreparable loss to the Institute. The Institute of Social Sciences organized a special meeting to discuss the life and work of George Fernandes (6 March 2019). Many leaders, scholars, eminent citizens and admirers of George Fernandes participated in the day-long programme. The volume *Legacy of George Fernandes* is based on the proceedings of that meeting. We hope this volume will keep alive the vision and mission of George Fernandes, the humble giant of India, for generations to come.

We are deeply grateful to Mr K.L. Thapar, founder and chairman, Asian Institute for Transport Development, an admirer of George Fernandes and an ardent supporter of his cause. Mr Thapar was Principal Advisor with the Planning Commission, Government of India. I am extremely thankful to him for his support to bring out three volumes in honour of George Saheb in 1990 on his 60th birthday. These include: 1. *George Fernandes Speaks*, 2. *Dignity for All*, 3. *Socialist Communist Interaction in India*. I owe a special debt of gratitude to Mr Thapar for his kind help for this publication.

I dedicate this volume to George Fernandes's inspiring memory, his heroic struggle and his lasting impact on Indian policy.

2 January 2020 **George Mathew**
New Delhi Chairman, Institute of Social Sciences

Contents

Introduction

Ash Narain Roy

In the age of illiberal conformism George Fernandes is even more relevant.

George Fernandes strode the national stage for over 50 years and continues to inspire millions of people. For the Institute, George Sahab was a patron and a well-wisher. He fits Alexander Pope's description:

"Thou wert our guide, philosopher and friend."

George Sahab holds a special place in the hearts and minds of the Indian people, one who fought against injustice and oppression. The Tibetans, Burmese, Sri Lankan Tamils and even Iranians are among his countless admirers. His Holiness the Dalai Lama, in his homage, described George Sahab as "a great humanitarian and believer in truth." He added that: "I am confident he will be reborn yet again to serve his country, in particular the cause of the less privileged people."

No single adjective or set of adjectives can adequately describe George Sahab. He had a passionate interest in matters relating to human freedom, justice and dignity. Democracy, to him, was a question of human dignity. And human dignity was political freedom.

A person of great warmth and intelligence, he mixed easily with both intellectuals and with the working class. He remained unwavering in his commitment towards the toiling masses, the Adivasis and the marginalized. His was the impassioned voice in the socialist labour movement.

George Sahab was a stormy petrel of Indian politics and a rebel without a pause, at times a rebel without a cause. He was driven by a strong social conscience and could captivate even those who did not share his ideology and worldviews.

Was he a trade union leader extraordinaire? Was he the epitome of anti-Congressism? Was he a fiery revolutionary? Was he an iconoclast? Was he a perennial dissenter? Was he a non-conformist? He was all rolled into one.

His nine Lok Sabha election wins are a testimony to his popularity, political genius, perseverance and killer instinct as a self-made leader.

He was a great parliamentarian. That he never received the best parliamentarian award is a sad commentary on the system of patronage.

George Sahab was known for his Spartan lifestyle—crumpled kurta-pyjamas, unkempt khadi chappals and his house open to everyone. We all know how he brought Mumbai to a standstill with the taxi drivers' strike. He also brought the railways to a halt.

He lit many fires and never allowed the one smouldering inside him to be extinguished.

His life was the stuff of a legend. His legacy will remain writ large on the national consciousness. Bihar was his *karmabhumi*. Some of his followers have come all the way from Muzaffarpur—Mohammad Ansari, Vijaya Choudhary and others.

Bihar was also the *karmabhumi* of other socialist giants like Acharya Kripalani and Madhu Limaye. Sri Surendra Kumar, former secretary of the Gandhi Peace Foundation, was a very close associate of George Sahab. As he says, George Sahab's decision to kick Coca Cola out was taken at Muzaffarpur which he represented in the Lok Sabha on various occasions. The district was reeling under severe drought. At a meeting the DM brought him a glass of Coca Cola which infuriated him.

George Sahab was a visionary railway and defence minister. He made Indians safe and strong. His role in preserving Indian democracy will also be remembered.

His role in Kashmir is not to be forgotten. He was the only Union Minister for Kashmir Affairs and lent his ear to the people in Kashmir in the most difficult period of history. He met many people and would even visit jails to interact with prisoners.

Even though part of the government, he remained an establishment outsider. George Sahab was a perennial dissenter.

He believed, without nurturing dissent, power tends towards authoritarianism. A democratic society cannot flourish in the absence of dissent.

Today he is even more relevant when India has moved towards aggressive consumerism and illiberal conformism.

At a time when the truth empire is on decline and when dissent is in short supply, we miss George Sahab. He believed that a chain is only as strong as its weakest link.

But his Socialist dreams lie in tatters. He was among the tallest Socialist leaders. We have lost the last Socialist giant. Not long ago, a proud Socialist International bestrode the global stage. What happened?

We also need to discuss this.

Historically, social democrats rose to power in tandem with a rising working class. Now, this once mighty force is shrinking along with manufacturing as a share of GDP. In the past 50 years, that portion has roughly dropped from 35 per cent to 15 per cent throughout the west. To put it brutally, the reformist left is losing its customer base which shows in all recent elections.

The socialist project seems to have crashed globally. Social democracy is on the ropes. It needs new vision. Some people in Europe talk of global social democracy.

Let me end by recalling the words of Robert Frost:

The Road Not Taken

I shall be telling this with a sigh
Somewhere ages and ages hence:
Two roads diverged in a wood, and I—
I took the one less travelled by,
And that has made all the difference.

The Life and Work of George Fernandes

Dick Gupwell

Introduction

On 29th January, George Mathew sent me an e-mail informing me that "Our dear friend, George Fernandes, died this morning". This was not altogether unexpected news as I knew that he had been very ill for a long time.

I had first met George Fernandes in 1978 and, over time, we had become good friends. I told Dr Mathew that, if there was an event to commemorate George Fernandes's life, then I would like to be there. So, here I am.

Initially, Dr Mathew had said that I should make a speech of "at least an hour". However, when I arrived from England, he told me that so many people would be attending the event, who wanted to speak, that I should limit my remarks to just twenty minutes. It is not easy to comment on the life and work of George Fernandes in only twenty minutes.

Therefore, I shall try briefly to summarize his life up to 1978 and then recount some of my personal reminiscences of this great man over the thirty or more years, during which I met him on a regular basis.

The Early Years, 1930-1967

George Fernandes was born on June 3, 1930. This was the birthday of the then King-Emperor, George V, which is probably why his parents called him George. George was born in Mangalore, an ancient port city in what is now Karnataka. Mangalore had been occupied by the Portuguese, in 1526, which explains why both his father, John Joseph's family name, Fernandes (spelt with an 's' rather than a Spanish 'z'), and his mother, Alice's maiden name, Pinto, are typically Portuguese names. It also explains why the family are Roman Catholics and why George was sent to a seminary in Bangalore, to train for the priesthood.

However, aged eighteen, George decided that this was not to be his destiny and, instead, he was determined to become a trade union activist, helping to organize the poor and exploited.

At first, he worked in his native Mangalore, alongside Placid d'Mello, organizing hotel workers and a strike of a road transport company's employees. Soon, however, he moved to Bombay, in 1949. Here, he began helping to organize such groups as the dock workers and the taxi drivers. In 1958, together with Madhu Limaye, George set up the Hind Mazdoor Panchayat (Indian Workers' Council) to bring these new trade unions together. In 1967, he also set up a Cooperative Bank.

Meanwhile, in 1934, Jayaprakash Narayan, Ram Manohar Lohia, Asoka Mehta and others had formed the Congress Socialist Party as a "ginger group" within the Indian National Congress and Madhu Limaye had joined this group in 1938. However, the Congress Socialists were weakened, in the late 1930s, by allowing "dual membership" with members of the Communist Party of India, which had been established, in 1925, and very much under the influence of Moscow. Then, during the Second World War, while many Socialist leaders were in prison for their participation in the "Quit India" movement, the Communists remained active, particularly after the Anglo-Soviet alliance, following the German attack on the Soviet Union, in June 1941. Thus, the Indian Communists were able to infiltrate the local Congress Socialist Party units and, often, to take them over.

After Indian independence from Britain, in 1947, the Congress Socialists had broken away from the Indian National Congress, in 1948, to form an independent Indian Socialist Party. Likewise, the Hindu Nationalist wing of the Congress, under Dr S.P. Mookerjee, had also left to form the Jana Sangh. In addition, another Congress group, under Jivatram Kripalani, had set up the Kisan Mazdoor Praja Party (Peasant and Working People's Party or KMPP).

George Fernandes had been introduced to Socialism in Mangalore and Bombay and became a party member, in 1949, under the influence of Jayaprakash Narayan, Dr Lohia and Madhu Limaye. In India's first General Election, in 1952, held under the British single-member constituency, "first past the post" electoral system, the Congress, under the leadership of the Congress Prime Minister, Jawaharlal Nehru, romped home with 47 million votes and 364 seats. In terms of votes, the Socialist Party came in second place, with 11 million votes, while the KMPP was third, with 6 million. However, in terms of seats won, the Socialists took only 12 and the KMPP 9, whereas the Communist Party, won 16 seats with only 3.4 million votes. The Jana Sangh gained 3 seats with just over 3 million votes.

To avoid the Communists becoming the main Opposition in Parliament, the Socialists and the KMPP decided to merge, becoming the Praja Socialist Party (PSP). However, internal disputes arose within the PSP, both over making seat arrangements either with the Congress (in Andhra Pradesh) or with the Communists (in Kerala) in state elections and then over the insistence of Asoka Mehta that the PSP work in cooperation with the Congress. Jayaprakash Narayan had retired from active politics, in 1954. Lohia, Limaye and others now broke away from the PSP, in 1955, and, the following year, established an independent Socialist Party to be "equidistant" from both the Congress and the Communists. However, this served to split the votes of the democratic left, in the General Elections of 1957 and 1962, helping to provide further massive majorities for the Congress.

Then, in 1964, Dr Lohia managed to reunite most of the Socialists in a new *Samyukta* (United) Socialist Party (SSP), although Asoka Mehta, Chandra Shekhar and others then moved to the Congress, while, in 1965, a few others also left the SSP to re-constitute the PSP.

George Fernandes Enters Politics, 1967-1975

George Fernandes was elected as a member of the Bombay Municipal Council, in 1961, and, in the General Election of 1967, he was elected to the Lok Sabha (the Lower House of India's Parliament) for the Samyutka Socialist Party, defeating the sitting Congress Member, the Railways Minister, S.K. Patil, in the Bombay South constituency. This earned him the nickname, "George the Giant Killer".

In that General Election, Ram Manohar Lohia had succeeded in arranging a series of electoral pacts (seat sharing arrangements) with other non-Communist parties, whereby the Congress was reduced to 283 seats, depriving the Congress of a comfortable working majority for the first time, while the opposition parties made considerable gains. However, the SSP then suffered the grievous loss of its leader, Dr Lohia, who died at the end of that year. George Fernandes was appointed as the SSP's General Secretary, in 1969.

Jawaharlal Nehru had died, in 1964, and his successor, Lal Bahadur Shastri, died in 1966. The Congress then elected Nehru's daughter, Indira Gandhi, as Congress leader and Prime Minister, although not without considerable controversy within the Party. Moreover, the Communist Party of India (CPI) had split, following the Sino-Soviet dispute, in 1964, with the formation of the Communist Party of India (Marxist). In addition, another Congress group, under Rajagopalachari, had broken away, in 1959, to form the Swatantra Party.

Then, following the 1967 Elections, the Chief Minister of Uttar Pradesh, Chaudhary Charan Singh, left the Congress to form the Bharatiya Kranti Dal (BKD), while, in 1969, the Chief Minister of Orissa, Biju Patnaik, did likewise, setting up the Uktal Congress. That same year, two other leading Congressmen, Morarji Desai and K. Kamaraj, formed the Organization Congress, Indira Gandhi responding by renaming her party the Ruling Congress (Congress-R).

However, this political success of the non-Congress opposition was short-lived. In the ensuing General Election, in 1971, while the Organization Congress (Congress-O), Swatantra, the Jana Sangh and the SSP campaigned together as the National Democratic Front (NDF), Indira Gandhi's Congress (R) won a great victory, gaining 352 seats against a total of only 49 seats for the NDF. The Socialists now suffered their worst electoral defeat thus far, the SSP winning only 3 seats, with just 2 for the PSP. Amongst the SSP losses was that of the Member for Bombay South, George Fernandes.

Immediately, the two Socialist parties began merger talks and, in July 1971, they united under the earlier name of the Indian Socialist Party, Karpoori Thakur of the SSP becoming Party President and

Mahdu Dandavate of the PSP, General Secretary. Then, in January 1973, George Fernandes was elected as President of the Socialist Party, while Surendra Mohan became General Secretary.

In October that year, George Fernandes was also elected as President of the All India Railwaymen's Federation. George then inherited a decision of the Railwaymen's Federation to go on strike for improved conditions. George tried to negotiate reasonable terms with the Ministry but he and thousands of others were arrested.

George Fernandes and the Socialist International

As Socialist Party President, George quickly returned the Socialist Party into full membership of the Socialist International. The old Socialist International, which had been founded in 1889, had foundered, first, over whether Socialists should support or oppose participation in the First World War, which broke out in 1914, and then, with the Bolshevik Revolution of 1917 in Russia and the formation of the Communist International, the following year, many Socialist parties split, some groups joining the Communist International and others joining a new Labour and Socialist International, set up in 1923.

This latter group was increasingly weakened by the formation of right-wing dictatorships under Horthy in Hungary (1920), Mussolini in Italy (1925), Salazar in Portugal (1932), Hitler in Germany (1933) and Franco in Spain (1938), amongst others, as well as Hitler's annexation of Austria (1938) and Czechoslovakia (1939), where these "democratic Socialist" parties were banned. Then, with the outbreak of the Second World War, in 1939, with the combined invasion of Poland by Hitler and Stalin, the dictator of Soviet Russia, and the subsequent occupation, between April and June 1940, of Denmark, Norway, the Netherlands, Belgium, Luxembourg and France, by Hitler's Nazi Germany, and Stalin's occupation of the Baltic republics, the Labour and Socialist International ceased to exist.

However, a series of meetings took place in London thereafter, which included Socialist parties-in-exile from the occupied countries, with a view to reconstituting the Socialist International. This process was accelerated with the ending of hostilities, in 1945, and Madhu Limaye represented the Congress Socialist Party at the Socialist Conference in Antwerp, held in late 1947. The new Socialist International was then established at the founding Congress in Frankfurt, in June 1951, with the Indian Socialist Party becoming a full member. However, between 1955 and 1969, the Indian Socialists were reduced to "Consultative" status. George Fernandes's decision for the reunited Socialist Party to resume full membership of the Socialist International and his active participation in its meetings, enabled him to meet many leading Socialist personalities, especially from Europe, which would later stand him in good stead.

Indira Gandhi's Imposition of Emergency Rule, 1975-1977

Mrs Gandhi's increasingly authoritarian style of government brought Jayaprakash Narayan out of retirement to lead a popular movement to preserve parliamentary democracy in India. An alliance, between the non-Communist parties opposing Mrs Gandhi's Congress (R), which included the Jana Sangh, the Lok Dal (recently formed by the merger of the BKD, the Uktal Congress and the Swatantra Party), the Socialists and Morarji Desai's Congress (O) was now brought together by Jayaprakash Narayan, in February 1975, and a Coordinating Committee was formed, which included Atal Bihari Vajpayee from the Jana Sangh, Asoke Mehta from the Congress (O), Raj Narain from the Lok Dal and with Madhu Limaye as Convenor. This alliance then heavily defeated Mrs Gandhi's "Ruling Congress" in the Gujarat State Elections, in June 1975. The same day, the Allahabad High Court found Mrs Gandhi guilty of malpractice during the 1971 General Election, in a case brought by Raj Narain, and banned her from standing in the next General Election, to be held in 1976.

A few days later, Mrs Gandhi announced a State of Emergency and ordered that all her political opponents be arrested and imprisoned. This included 25,000 senior and middle-ranking Socialist Party activists but George Fernandes managed to evade capture for a year. In their attempts to find him, Mrs Gandhi's police stooped to torturing George's brother, Lawrence, and harassing his other brothers and his now elderly mother, Alice, to no avail.

It was at this point that I became involved.

In early 1976, I was appointed as a Political Advisor in the

Secretariat of the Socialist Group in the European Parliament. Prior to that, I had worked at the International Confederation of Free Trade Unions (ICFTU), from 1972 to 1974, and as an Administrator in the General Secretariat of the Commission of the European Communities, from 1974 to 1976, both in Brussels.

By the summer of 1976, I had been reading articles in the journal of the Socialist International, *Socialist Affairs*, about Mrs Gandhi's Emergency Rule and the arrest of the leaders of the Indian Socialist Party, including, in June 1976, George Fernandes. I had also read how many European Socialist leaders, including Willy Brandt, the former Chancellor of Germany and the then President of the Socialist International, Bruno Kriesky, the Austrian Chancellor, Olaf Palme, the Swedish Prime Minister, Hans Janitschek, the Secretary General of the Socialist International, and Mario Soares, the Portuguese Socialist Party leader, had warned Mrs Gandhi that no harm should come to George Fernandes.

Also, at that time, Monsieur Ortoli, the President of the European Commission, had visited New Delhi to hold discussions with the Government of India about future trade relations, which, at that time, were based on the Commercial Cooperation Agreement of 1973. At a joint press conference with Mrs Gandhi, Monsieur Ortoli had spoken of the desirability of strengthening these trade relations.

I felt that, in view of Mrs Gandhi's Emergency Rule, this was not an appropriate time to be thinking of strengthening trade relations with India. Therefore, I discussed with a Socialist Member of the European Parliament (MEP) from the Netherlands, Schelto Patijn, the possibility of raising this issue in Parliament and Mr Patijn obtained the agreement of the Socialist Group to table an Oral Question with Debate to the Commission.

In order to be adequately prepared for the forthcoming debate, I contacted the Socialist International in London, who put me in touch with M.S. Hoda, who had been a leading member of the Railwaymen's Federation and who was now working with the International Transport Workers' Federation in London. Surur Hoda also acted as the representative of the Indian Socialist Party in London and he provided me with all the information I required.

In fact, the debate in the European Parliament took place

only a few weeks before Mrs Gandhi held the postponed General Election, which was in March 1977. In the debate, the name of George Fernandes featured prominently in Mr Patijn's speech.

In order to contest the General Election, the main non-Communist opposition parties, who had earlier come together to fight the Gujarat State election, agreed not merely to continue their alliance but actually to merge their parties into a new Janata (People's) Party, which was also joined by a new group under Jagjivan Ram, the Congress for Democracy, which had recently left the Congress (R). Both George Fernandes and Surendra Mohan had initially (i.e. before the Emergency) been opposed to an outright merger of the parties, fearing that this would lead to a lasting disappearance of an independent Socialist Party. However, while this was a major sacrifice for each of the parties, by 1977, the stakes of returning India to parliamentary democracy were considered by all to be too high to do otherwise.

The Janata Government: George Fernandes as Industry Minister, 1977-1979

The result was the defeat of Mrs Gandhi's Ruling Congress and a victory for the Janata Party, the Janata/Congress for Democracy alliance winning 298 seats against 153 for the Congress (R). Thus, a new government was formed under Morarji Desai and George Fernandes was appointed as Minister for Industry. Other leading Socialists also obtained Cabinet positions, including Mahdu Dandavate as Railways Minister. Atal Bihari Vajpayee was appointed at External Affairs, Charan Singh at Home Affairs and Jagjivan Ram at Defence. Madhu Limaye was Janata Party General Secretary. Although only in a minority, in what was, in effect, a coalition government, this was the first time that Indian Socialists had been able to exert a direct influence on government policy.

In 1978, George Fernandes visited Brussels, where he held discussions with the European Commission on trade relations. He also visited the European Parliament, then in session in Luxembourg, accompanied by Lalit Mansingh from the Indian Embassy in Brussels, who introduced me to George and we had tea in the Members' Bar.

As Industry Minister, George was able to implement some

of his ideas on economic policy, particularly to tackle the serious under-investment in the rural economy. Indeed, this emphasis on satisfying the needs of the rural sector had been a key issue for Socialists like Lohia and Limaye and had also been a principal concern of Mahatma Gandhi himself. By contrast, Nehru and the Congress were influenced by the centralized economic planning model of the Soviet Union, with its emphasis on developing heavy industry.

As Industry Minister, George Fernandes is, perhaps, best remembered for his dispute with the Coca Cola Company of the United States. George was, in general, suspicious of the activities of large multinational corporations. In the case of Coca Cola, he wanted that company to source much of its raw materials, for the Coca Cola sold in India, from local Indian sources, so as to generate local employment, given that India produced most of the ingredients required. When the Coca Cola Company flatly refused to consider this, George told them that they could no longer operate in India. Instead, George established a factory to produce a Cola drink as a substitute, using only home-grown raw materials. He called this "77", after the year of the Janata Party's election victory. However, most people knew it as "George Cola".

Mrs Gandhi's defeat led to a further split in her Congress (R) Party, in 1978, as three former Congress Chief Ministers, Devaraj Urs (Karnataka), Y.B. Chavan (Maharashtra) and Brahmanand Reddy (Andhra Pradesh) broke away to form the Congress (U), Mrs Gandhi responding by renaming her party the Indira Congress or Congress(I). The Janata Government broke up, in 1979, due to intractable differences over policy, particularly between the Socialist and Lok Dal factions, who wished to defend India's secular traditions, on the one hand, and, on the other, the Jana Sangh faction and their emphasis on pursuing their Hindu nationalist communal policies, something for which Morarji Desai, a strictly orthodox Hindu, had some sympathy. In May 1979, Madhu Limaye convened a meeting of those, who were prepared to fight against the "twin dangers" of authoritarianism, as represented by the Congress (I), and the communalism of the Jana Sangh faction.

The crisis came in July 1979. First, Raj Narain and a few others left the Janata Party to form the Janata (Secular) Party. Y.B. Chavan then tabled a Motion of No Confidence in the Desai Government. In the debate, on July 12th, George Fernandes spoke in defence of the Janata Government's work, especially as regards its economic policy. However, after talking to Madhu Limaye, he then tendered his resignation the following day and the Desai Government fell. Madhu had convinced George that, as a Christian, he could not support a government, whose policies would discriminate against both Muslims and Christians.

For the remainder of 1979, a minority government was formed under Charan Singh but Mrs Gandhi's Indira Congress was returned to power in the General Election, held in January 1980, the Congress (I) winning 351 seats, an alliance between the reconstituted Lok Dal, under Charan Singh, and the Congress (U) winning 54 seats, and the Janata Party, 34 seats, while the two Communist parties and their allies won 54 seats. George Fernandes retained his seat in the Lok Sabha and joined the reconstituted Lok Dal Party, along with some of the Socialists (mostly ex-SSP), while other former members of the Socialist Party (mainly ex-PSP) chose to remain with the Janata Party. At the end of 1980, the Jana Sangh faction also left the Janata Party and reconstituted itself as the Bharatiya Janata Party (BJP).

European Parliament Delegations to India

In November 1981, the European Parliament, which had been directly elected by the citizens of the European Communities for the first time, in 1979, sent its first-ever delegation to India to meet the Indian Parliament and I was asked to accompany the delegation and its two Socialist Members. I wrote to George Fernandes to ask if he could arrange a separate meeting with some Indian Socialists and he suggested that I arrive a few days in advance of the delegation to finalize this.

This I did, and I was met at the airport and taken to George's house in Tuglaq Crescent, where lunch was served in the lawn. That evening, after I had rested, George and Leila took me to a wedding party. This was my first day in India. The delegation's meetings took place, which included a meeting with Mrs Gandhi. However, the highlight for me was a dinner given at George Fernandes's house for the two Socialist MEPs and myself, where the guest of honour was Biju Patnaik.

George also arranged for me to be interviewed by a friend of his, who worked for the Press Trust of India, and his article about the delegation meetings then appeared in several newspapers, and in Bombay, I was able to meet some of George's trade union leaders.

In this way, George and I became friends. He would stay at my house, when he visited Belgium, and I was always welcome to stay at his house, when I was in Delhi. This gave us many opportunities to discuss his views on Indian politics. We also met sometimes in London with our mutual friend, Surur Hoda.

George again lost his seat in the Lok Sabha in the General Election of 1984, which followed Mrs Gandhi's assassination by her Sikh bodyguards, after Operation Blue Star (the military operation to remove Sant Jarnail Singh Bhindranwale and his Sikh militant supporters from the Golden Temple in Amritsar), and the huge sympathy vote won by her son, Rajiv Gandhi. The result was Congress (I) 404 seats, Congress Socialist Party (ex-Congress-U) 4 seats, BJP 2 seats, Janata 10 seats, Lok Dal 3 seats, CPI (M) 22 and CPI 6 seats.

I now temporarily lost touch with George and, on my next visit to India, I went to Tuglaq Cresent to be told that he had moved to Haus Khaz. There, I managed to find George's house but he was out. However, I met his assistant, Ravi Nair, who soon became another friend.

I later accompanied another European Parliament Delegation to India in the spring of 1986. This time, George Fernandes arranged for our Socialist Members to visit a new, left-leaning Institute, which had recently been established by a certain Dr George Mathew. This, of course, was the Institute of Social Sciences, then housed in its small home in Safdarjang Enclave. On another occasion, George Fernandes also arranged for me to have a long discussion with his friend, Madhu Limaye, which was most enlightening. Madhu kindly gave me a copy of his book, *Politics After Freedom*.

George Fernandes and the Janata Dal, 1979-1989

In opposition and out of Parliament, George Fernandes worked tirelessly to bring about the reunification of the progressive forces in the Lok Dal and what remained of the Janata Party. This was finally achieved in October 1988, the merged party adopting the name Janata Dal. Moreover, there were further defections from the Congress (I) Party, with the Jan Morcha being formed by V.P. Singh and others. George was also much involved with unearthing the details of the Bofors scandal, which involved "kickbacks" being paid by the Swedish arms manufacturer for the contract to supply field guns to India. At our various meetings, mostly in Europe, George would discuss the progress that he was making on these issues and keep me abreast of developments.

In addition, on the occasion of another visit of the Delegation of the European Parliament, George Fernandes arranged for another of our Socialist MEPs, George Stevenson, and me to attend a conference of the Janata Dal held near Pune, where we met such leading figures as Chandra Shekhar and Madhu Dandavate.

As it happened, Rajiv Gandhi failed to win a majority in the General Election, held in November 1989. The Congress (I) won 197 seats as against 143 for the Janata Dal/Jan Morcha alliance (which campaigned as the "National Front"), 85 for the BJP, 33 for the CPI (M) and 12 for the CPI. The Janata Dal, in alliance with the Jan Morcha, were now able to form a minority government, with V.P. Singh as Prime Minister, and with outside support in the Lok Sabha from the BJP and the Communists.

George Fernandes was now, once again, a Member of the Lok Sabha, where he would remain for the next twenty years, now representing a constituency in Bihar. He was appointed as Railways Minister and, for a short time, he was also given responsibility for the deteriorating situation in Kashmir. V.P. Singh was Prime Minister and also held the Defence portfolio, while Devi Lal (ex-Lok Dal) was Deputy Prime Minister with the Agriculture portfolio. M.M. Syed and I.K. Gujral (both from the Jan Morcha) took Home Affairs and External Affairs respectively and Mahdu Dandavate was given Finance.

The Janata Dal/National Front Government: George Fernandes as Railways Minister, 1989-1991

George's greatest success as Railways Minister was to launch the building of the Konkan Railway, to link Bombay via Goa with Mangalore along the coast, thus greatly reducing the length of the existing journey by the inland route. This had been a project under consideration for some time but the difficulties of the terrain meant that it had never been realized. George's idea (as he explained it to me) was for construction to begin in several places at once. He realized that he would not remain as Minister for long but, in this way, with so many contractors involved, it would become too expensive to cancel the project.

The Konkan Railway now stands as testimony both to the quality of Indian engineering and to George Fernandes's determination and foresight.

During his short time with responsibility for Kashmir, George visited the Valley and met the local youth. He understood that much of the militancy was due to the serious problem of youth unemployment. The natural outlet from the Vale of Kashmir is into Pakistan and, during the winter months, the mountainous road to the rest of India is frequently blocked by snow. George pushed for planning to be undertaken to drive a railway through the mountains, to enable produce from Kashmir to be exported to the rest of India all year round and, thus, help to stimulate the local economy. This project is only now being completed.

It did not take long for the BJP to withdraw its support from the Government of V.P. Singh over communal issues. In November 1990, V.P. Singh resigned and a group of sixty Janata Dal MPs, led by Chandra Shekhar and Devi Lal, broke away to form the Janata Dal (Socialist) Party (or Samajwadi Janata Dal) and, initially, were able to form a government, with Chandra Shekhar as Prime Minister and with Congress (I) support. However, the Congress (I) provoked fresh elections, in June 1991, and was again in power, the Congress (I) winning 244 seats, the BJP 120 and the Janata Dal only 59. During the campaign, Rajiv Gandhi had been assassinated by a militant of the Tamil Tigers from Sri Lanka and the new government was led by P.V. Narasimha Rao.

The Collapse of the Janata Dal, 1991-1998

Thereafter, the Janata Dal steadily disintegrated and the BJP became the main rival to the Congress. In October 1992, Mulayam Singh Yadav, the Janata Dal Chief Minister of Uttar Pradesh from December 1989 to June 1991, now also broke from the Janata Dal and formed the Samajwadi Party and was re-elected as Chief Minister, in December 1993. Meanwhile, George Fernandes, who had long hoped to revive a distinct Socialist Party, had been telling me that either he would have to make the Janata Dal into something more closely resembling a democratic socialist party or he would have to reconstitute an independent Socialist Party. In the period before 1994, he had organized several conferences bringing together grassroots Socialists sharing this view.

Things came to a head in 1994. When V.P. Singh stepped down as leader of the Janata Dal parliamentary party that year, the party replaced him with Sharad Yadav, although George Fernandes was by far the more senior sitting member in Parliament. Sharad Yadav had been supported by his co-member of the Yadav (or cowherd) caste, Laloo Prasad Yadav, the Janata Dal Chief Minister of Bihar, since March 1990. Then, with state elections due in Bihar, in 1995, George felt that he could not, in all conscience, fight on the same party ticket as Laloo Prasad Yadav, who had blatantly run the state in a corrupt manner sidelining his professional civil servants in favour of his caste cronies. As a result, George Fernandes, together with Nitish Kumar (a junior Minister for Agriculture under V.P. Singh), took the plunge and set up the Samata (or Equality) Party to contest the state elections independently.

However, the democratic left was now too divided to make Samata more than a marginal electoral force on its own. To make any serious impression, the party would have to attract the support of the large Muslim minority but failed to do so. Laloo Prasad Yadav retained a majority of seats and remained as Chief Minister.

The next hurdle came in the lead up to the General Election, due in 1996. George Fernandes wanted the Samata Party to campaign in alliance with the Janata Dal but this was now blocked by Biju Patnaik, who had been the Janata Dal Chief Minister of Orissa since 1990. However, in the Orissa State elections, in 1995, Rabi Ray, who had been elected as Speaker of the Lok Sabha, in 1991, formed the Orissa branch of the Samata Party, which contested against Patnaik's Janata Dal. The Janata Dal vote share fell from 53.7 per cent to 35.7 per cent and the party lost two-thirds of its seats, allowing the Congress (I) to form the next state government (although the Samata vote share was a mere 0.3 per cent). The upshot was that, from 1996, the Samata Party contested elections in alliance with the BJP.

The result of the 1996 General Election was a stalemate. The Congress (I) lost its majority and the BJP emerged as the largest party, with Samata winning over 7 million votes and 8 Lok Sabha seats. Against this, an alliance between the Janata Dal, the Samajwadi Party and a regional party from Andhra Pradesh, the Telugu Desam, won a total of 79 seats (as against 161 for the BJP and 140 for the Congress-I). A minority government was now formed under H.D. Deve Gowda, hitherto the Janata Dal Chief Minister of Karnataka, with outside support from the Congress (I). However, in April 1997, the Congress (I) leader, Sitaram Kesri, obliged Deve Gowda to stand down and he was succeeded by I.K. Gujral. However, Gujral subsequently refused to follow the dictates of Mr Kesri and fresh elections were held early in 1998.

By now, the Janata Dal had suffered further splits. In February 1997, the Janata Dal leaders, Deve Gowda and Sharad Yadav, ousted Ramakrishna Hegde (a former Janata Chief Minister of Karnataka), who then formed the Lok Shakti Party. Shortly thereafter, Laloo Prasad Yadav, by then facing serious corruption charges, was also expelled and, in turn, Laloo formed the Rashtriya Janata Dal (RJD). Then, following the death of Biju Patnaik, in April 1997, his son, Naveen, took over the leadership of the Janata Dal in Orissa and, when the party refused to allow him to ally with the BJP, he broke away to form the Biju Janata Dal at the end of that year.

Thus, when the next General Election was held, the BJP campaigned in alliance with three former Janata Dalgroups—the Samata Party, the Lok Shakti and the Biju Janata Dal (BJD), as well as with several regional parties—in a National Democratic Alliance (NDA). As for the rest of the former Janata Dal, the rump of the party campaigned with the CPI and the CPI (M), while the RJD fought in alliance with the Bahajun Samaj Party (which represented the lowest castes, particularly in Uttar Pradesh), and the Samajwadi Party campaigned on its own.

The result was a clear victory for the NDA. The BJP won 182 seats, Samata 12, the BJD 9, the Lok Shakti 3 and the other allies a further 48 seats. Against this, the Congress (I) and its allies won 144 seats. The rump of the Janata Dal was reduced to only 6 seats, the RJD won 17 seats and the Samajwadi Party 20 seats.

Thus, a new government was formed by the parties of the

National Democratic Alliance under the leadership of the BJP President, the moderate Atal Bihari Vajpayee, as Prime Minister. George Fernandes was appointed as Defence Minister but he was also the Convenor of the NDA and was able to exert sufficient influence to restrain the BJP from attempting to implement its radical communal policies. Yashwant Sinha, a former Janata Dal politician (at one time George's election agent in Bihar), who had since joined the BJP, became Finance Minister, while Ramakrishna Hegde became Commerce Minister, Naveen Patnaik received Steel and Mines and Nitish Kumar, Railways.

Some of George Fernandes's Other Interests

However, before looking at George's role as Defence Minister, I have to back-track a bit.

First, I want to say that George Mathew's initiative to set up the Institute of Social Sciences (ISS), which he did with the warm support of George Fernandes, gave me the idea, which led to the creation, in 1989, of what is now the European Institute for Asian Studies in Brussels. Among the founder members was Malcolm Subhan, then the Brussels correspondent of the *Economic Times* of India. Our mutual friend, Surur Hoda, was an early member of our Board and remained so until his death in 2003. George Fernandes spoke at our Institute on several occasions and we made him an Honorary Member.

In turn, Surur Hoda invited me to join the Board of his charity organization, the India Development Group (UK), which, since the 1970s, has been involved in rural development projects in India, based on the philosophy of Dr E.F. Schumacher, author of the bestselling book, *Small is Beautiful or Economics as if People Mattered,* ideas similar to those held by George Fernandes. Indeed, George Fernandes was always a strong supporter of the IDG, which now continues to operate under the name of the Jeevika Trust.

In addition, George was a not infrequent visitor to meetings of the Socialist Group in the European Parliament, where he was always made welcome. For example, he participated in the Group's Round-Table discussion on Kashmir, organized in Brussels, in October 1993. Other participants from India included Dr Farooq Abdullah, who had served as Chief Minister of Jammu and Kashmir State, and Ravi Nair, now leading the South Asia Human Rights Documentation Centre.

Also, George Fernandes and Madhu Dandavate represented Indian Socialism at the meeting of the Socialist International's Asia-Pacific Committee, in Kathmandu, in December 1993. I stayed at George's house, now at Krishna Menon Marg, both on the way there and on the way back.

George Fernandes as Minister of Defence, 1998-2004

So, to return to George's time as Defence Minister, several points should be made here.

First, there was the nuclear test, carried out in May 1998. This did not come as a surprise to me as, only a few days beforehand, Muchkund Dubey, a senior Indian official, had given a talk at our Institute in Brussels, in which he had spoken about the failure of successive Indian governments to obtain an agreement in favour of comprehensive international nuclear disarmament, while India was increasingly threatened by China's growing nuclear arsenal.

Anyway, nuclear matters fell within the competence of the Prime Minister and not the Minister of Defence and George, who had been a consistent opponent of India acquiring nuclear weapons, had given Dr Mathew an assurance, up to the last minute, that he would speak at a Conference, which ISS was holding in Calicut and Cochin, to mark the 500th anniversary of the arrival of Vasco da Gama in India. However, on my way to that Conference, I spotted a sign painted on a wall, which read, "By George, he did it", which made me think that many people wrongly believed that George, rather than Mr Vajpayee, had been responsible.

Second was George's determination to clear up the problem of corruption within the Defence Ministry over arms procurement (the same issue, which had led V.P. Singh to leave Rajiv Gandhi's Congress (I) Government).

Third was his successful attempts to ensure that India's armed forces were properly equipped with modern weaponry. This included procuring fighter aircraft for the Air Force and a modern aircraft carrier for the Navy.

His major achievement, however, was his reaction to the Kargil crisis, which began in April 1999, when Pakistani "intruders" crossed the Line of Control and illegally occupied the heights above the Kargil Valley. He determined that India's military response should be limited to repulsing the Pakistani forces and that the conflict should not be widened, while, at the same time, ensuring that international diplomatic pressure was exerted on Pakistan to desist. By July, the operation was successfully concluded.

Meanwhile, in April 1999, the NDA's regional ally from Tamil Nadu left the government and fresh elections were held in October. By this time, Sharad Yadav had decided that the rump of the Janata Dal should also ally with the NDA. Deve Gowda, however, disagreed and now broke away to form the Janata Dal (Secular) Party or JD(S). George Fernandes now proposed that all the former Janata Dal groups within the NDA should unite to form a large counterweight to the BJP. Sharad Yadav agreed but neither Naveen Patnaik, nor Ramakrishna Hegde were prepared to merge their parties. The same applied to Om Prakash Chautala (the son of Devi Lal) who had reconstituted the Lok Dal in Haryana and had also joined the NDA. Thus, the new Janata Dal (United) Party or JD(U), was limited to the Janata Dal and Samata parties, whose bilateral relations remained uneasy for some time.

The outcome of the 1999 General Election was that the BJP retained 182 seats. The BJP's allies in the NDA won a further 83 seats, of which the JD(U) won 21, the BJD 10 and the Lok Dal 2, although the Lok Shakti lost all its seats. The NDA was also supported by the Telugu Desam from Andhra Pradesh, who won a further 29 seats. Against this, the Congress (I) won 114 seats and its allies a further 32 seats, of which the RJD gained 7 seats. The Samajwadi Party again campaigned independently, winning 26 seats, as did the JD(S) and Chandra Shekhar's Samajwadi Janata Party, which won one each. This enabled the NDA to govern for a further five years.

George Fernandes's other main achievement was to get close to, and earn the respect of, the service men and women of India's armed forces. For this, he camped with the soldiers on the icy mountains along the Line of Control, he flew with pilots in jet fighters and even went under the sea in submarines.

Indeed, I have a photograph of George at home, which he gave me while he was Defence Minister. George is wearing his usual *kurta pyjamas* but he is also wearing a life jacket, because he has just landed on the flight deck of an Indian destroyer, which is steaming at sea, in company with a second destroyer, probably at about twenty knots. He explained to me that, after visiting the ship's company of the first destroyer, the captain of the other destroyer asked if the Minister would also visit his ship. George happily agreed and was then hauled across the foaming sea between the two warships on a "bosun's chair". This was, surely, a valiant act for a man of over seventy years of age.

Even as Defence Minister, George Fernandes was reluctant to have any guards to protect him either at home or on visits. He once complained to me that many Ministers were reluctant to travel, especially to outlying towns and villages, without a *posse* of black-uniformed security guards and crates of bottled mineral water in the boot of the ministerial car. He told me, "These days, it's all Black Cats and Bisleri!"

Finally, George's time as Defence Minister was brought to a sad end by the "Tehelka Affair". While a few senior officers in the Ministry were found guilty of accepting bribes and one Samata Party official was also implicated (George described this as "conmen dealing with a conman"), George, himself, was exonerated of any blame by the official commission of inquiry. Indeed, it would have been entirely out of keeping with George's character ever to be involved with any such thing. He preferred the simple life and was entirely unpretentious, with little or no interest in material gain. Nevertheless, he was pursued relentlessly by the Congress Party and its leader, Sonia Gandhi, probably out of revenge for George's unearthing of the Bofors affair during the rule of her late husband, Rajiv.

The Twilight Years of George Fernandes

In the General Election of 2004, the NDA lost its majority. The BJP won 138 seats and its allies a further 41 seats, of which the JD(U) gained 8 seats and the BJD 11. George Fernandes retained his seat in Bihar. The Congress (I) now won 145 seats and its allies another 73 seats (of which the RJD won 24). Campaigning independently, the Samajwadi Party won 36 seats, the JD(S) 3 and the Lok Dal in Uttar Pradesh (led by Charan Singh's son, Ajit Singh) 1 seat (although the Haryana Lok Dal lost all its seats).

A new Congress-led Government was now formed as the United Progressive Alliance under Manmohan Singh (who had earlier served as Finance Minister under Narasimha Rao). Laloo Prasad Yadav was appointed as Railways Minister. However, Sonia Gandhi exerted considerable influence on government policy from outside the Cabinet.

For his last term in the Lok Sabha, George Fernandes was once again in opposition. Sadly, his mental faculties now began to fail him. Before long, he was diagnosed with Alzheimer's disease. When I visited him, in 2007, I could tell that he had slowed down somewhat. Nevertheless, he invited me to join him at a demonstration, where villagers were protesting against being displaced, in order to clear land for the expansion of Delhi's international airport, without being given reasonable compensation. George made a speech and I noted that much of the old fire was still there. However, two years later, during my next visit to Delhi, it was clear that his condition had deteriorated considerably.

In the run-up to the General Election of 2009, Nitish Kumar, the leader of the JD(U), who had become Chief Minister of Bihar, in October 2005, considered that George should no longer stand for election to the Lok Sabha and that, instead, a seat could be given to him in the upper house of Parliament, the Rajya Sabha. However, George's *entourage* arranged for him to stand as an Independent in his Bihar constituency against the official JD(U) candidate and he was defeated by a large majority. Nevertheless, Nitish Kumar still provided him (temporarily at least) with a Rajya Sabha seat but it was clear that George was no longer able to play any active part in politics.

This was a tragic end to what had been a long and brilliant political career.

In the 2009 General Election, Nitish Kumar's JD(U) had again campaigned as part of the National Democratic Alliance, winning 20 seats (the BJP won 116 seats), as did Ajit Singh's Lok Dal in Uttar Pradesh (RLD), which now won 5 seats under the NDA umbrella (the NDA's other partners winning 18 seats). Against this, the Congress won 206 seats and its United Democratic Alliance (UDA) partners a further 52 seats. Thus, Manmohan Singh was able to continue as Prime Minister for another five years.

As for the other former Janata Dal offshoots, there had been a number of developments. First, in 2006, there had been a split in the JD(S). Deve Gowda wished for the party now to ally with the Congress but he was expelled by Surendra Mohan and others, who wished the party to remain independent. Then, shortly prior to the general election, Naveen Patnaik's BJD decided to leave the NDA, as did the Haryana Lok Dal, and campaigned as part of a "Third Front", which included both Communist parties (CPI and CPI-M) and their far left allies, the BJD, the JD(S), as well as the BSP and certain regional parties, winning a total of 79 seats, while the Samajwadi Party continued to contest independently of all three groups.

Ensuring the Legacy of George Fernandes

It is now important that the legacy of George Fernandes be maintained, both as an inspiring leader of Democratic Socialism in India and as a great internationalist.

He was a lifelong defender of the interests of the poor, the weak and the downtrodden. He believed that no man or woman in India should live without basic human dignity. He understood that the underprivileged masses in India could only obtain strength through organization and unity. His attempts to create and maintain a strong political movement of the progressive democratic left ultimately failed because, too often, the rival ambitions of individual leaders led to successive splits and divisions. However, if India is not, in future, to be run largely in the interests of an increasingly rich, but small, property-owning minority, to the detriment of the great majority, such unity will have to be created, possibly on the basis of an association or federation of individual progressive democratic parties from India's states, in order to match the strength of the main "national" political parties, the BJP and the Congress.

After the 2004 General Election, the moderate Atal Bihari Vajpayee had retired and was replaced by the more hardline L.K. Advani, who led the BJP into another defeat, in 2009. Then, in the run-up to the 2014 General Election, the BJP chose Narendra Modi as its candidate to lead the party. Modi's reputation, as Chief Minister of Gujarat, had been tarnished as a result of the serious communal violence, in 2002. Nitish Kumar and the JD(U) now left the NDA. The Samajwadi Party, the JD(U), the JD(S) and the BJD were involved in talks with the two Communist parties, as well as several other parties, with a view to forming a "Third Front" independent of both the NDA and the UPA but these were inconclusive and no overall seat arrangement was made. The RJD remained in the UPA. The result was a great victory for the BJP, which won 282 seats, despite gaining only 31 per cent of the votes, and its allies a further 54 seats. The Congress, now led by Sonia Gandhi's son, Rahul, won only 44 seats with 19.5 per cent of the votes. The RJD won 3 seats and other UPA allies another 12 seats. Apart from the BJD, which won 20 seats, the other former Janata Dal parties fared poorly (Samajwadi 5, JD(U) 2 and JD(S) 2 seats).

However, in April 2015, the Samajwadi Party, the JD(U), the RJD, the JD(S), the Lok Dal and the Samajwadi Janata Party agreed to combine together both within and outside Parliament, although the BJD remained aloof. In November that year, the JD(U) and the RJD sank their long-standing differences and campaigned together in the Bihar State elections in a Grand Alliance (Mahagathabandhan) but insisted on also bringing in the Congress. The Samajwadi Party initially wanted to join this alliance but refrained after not being allocated enough seats. Nevertheless, it resulted in a substantial defeat for the BJP.

As for the forthcoming General Election, to be held in April and May in 2019, the former Janata Dal parties have again failed to combine into a single electoral force. The JD(U) has re-joined the BJP-led NDA, the RJD and the JD(S) are with the Congress-led UPA, the Samajwadi Party and the Uttar Pradesh Lok Dal have combined with the BSP in the Mahagathabandhan, while the BJD is fighting independently in Odisha (the new name for Orissa).

Thus, George Fernandes's long-held belief in the need for unity amongst the progressive democratic forces in India is still far from being realized. However, if the parties, which formerly belonged to the undivided Janata Dal, could sink their regional differences and come together, perhaps in alliance with such parties as the Trinamool Congress of Mamata Banerjee, in West Bengal, they could well become a viable rival to both the BJP and the Congress.

George Fernandes also believed that, in terms of international relations, India should play a positive role in world affairs and live in peaceful cooperation with its neighbours. He was a strong supporter of South Asian regional cooperation through SAARC and believed that the search for greater understanding by both sides would help to resolve the recurring tensions with Pakistan.

George remained close to the member parties of the Socialist International until 1995, taking part in the SI Council's meetings in Budapest, in December 1994, and Cape Town, in July 1995. Thereafter, however, the SI preferred to work with what remained of the Janata Dal and, at the Council meeting in Brussels, at the end of 1995, S.R. Bommai participated, while at the meeting in Delhi, in November 1997, Deve Gowda, Sharad Yadav, Madhu Dandavate and Surendra Mohan were all present.

Thereafter, when the Janata Dal split again, one faction joining the JD(U) and the other becoming the JD(S), the SI maintained relations with the latter until 2007. That year, the SI began to turn towards the Congress and, by December 2014, the Congress was admitted as a Full Member of the International. George Fernandes would certainly have been opposed to such a move.

However, in May 2013, a new international organization, the Progressive Alliance, was established in Leipzig, following a number of meetings beginning the previous year. This step was taken because some (particularly European) Democratic Socialist parties, led by the Social Democratic Party of Germany (SPD), had become frustrated by the SI's policy of recruiting some parties with dubious democratic credentials. The Congress has also joined the Progressive Alliance but so also has the Samajwadi Party. It would be a positive development if other Janata Dal offshoots would became associated with the Progressive Alliance. This would enable them to develop useful relations with the European Union's Party of European Socialists (PES), whose Group of Socialists and Democrats is the second largest political formation in the European Parliament, something from which George Fernandes had benefited for many years.

In conclusion, therefore, it is important that those, who knew and admired George Fernandes, ensure that the memory of his work and his fundamental humanity be passed on to the next generation, in whose hands the future of India will lie.

To End with an Anecdote

On one occasion, in London, Surur Hoda and his Italian wife, Elizabeth, invited George Fernandes and me for a dinner at the Royal Overseas League. George recounted to us how he had met President Gaddafi of Libya. My recollection is that this meeting had taken place while George was Industry Minister in the Government of Morarji Desai. The Cabinet had been discussing how India might obtain an increase in development aid and someone mentioned that Libya, with its vast oil and gas reserves, might be a useful source. It was agreed that George should be sent to meet President Gaddafi.

This mission was arranged and George flew to Tripoli. Once there, he was kept waiting in his hotel for three days until word came that the President was ready to meet him. George was taken to the vast Presidential Palace. Inside the palace was a large courtyard and, in the middle of the courtyard there was a large Arab-style tent. George was ushered into the tent and asked to sit on a cushion on a carpet, while President Gadhafi was seated on a raised platform.

George had thought carefully about to how he would address the President and decided to address him as "Brother Gaddafi". After some initial pleasantries, George raised the subject of development aid. President Gaddafi observed that, regarding South Asia, Libya only provided aid to its Muslim brothers in Pakistan. He then asked George, "Can you give me one reason why I should give aid to India?" George replied, "Brother Gaddafi, I can give you 150 million reasons", this being approximately India's Muslim population at that time. George then returned to Delhi with a promise to provide India with several hundred million dollars of aid.

This anecdote is a good example of George Fernandes's character.

Some Aspects of the Life and Legacy of George Fernandes

Anand Kumar

Introduction

George Fernandes (June 3, 1930–January 29, 2019), was one of the most charismatic leaders of India and Asia who was equally popular among the urban workers, rural masses, the middle classes, students and youth. He was one of the last icons of Indian democracy with a following all over the country beyond the prevailing barriers of region, religion and languages. He generated long lasting bonds of loyalty across the social categories and also created deep hostility among the adversaries.

He was a rare socialist leader who excelled in working class movements as well as parliamentary politics as a non-Congress politician. It included the long regime of Prime Minister Indira Gandhi from 1966 to 1984, with a gap of three years of Janata Party rule ('77-'79). He was elected 8 times to the Indian Parliament between 1967 and 2014.

He began his public life in the early 1960s as a modest councillor of the Mumbai Municipal Corporation and climbed, in the next ten years, to become a globally known socialist fighter for democracy and union minister in 1977 as he was an attractive combination of conviction and courage. He served with distinction in the cabinets of four Prime Ministers: Morarji Desai, Charan Singh, V.P. Singh and Atal Bihari Vajpayee. Obviously, he had his share of puzzling contradictions in such an illustrious public life as his public activities defied categorization.

George Fernandes made his mark primarily as a courageous socialist leader who often risked his all for the freedom and rights of the common citizens. He personified a rare capacity to take courage in both hands to challenge the might of authority and rally support around a very inspiring vision. I had the privilege of knowing and observing him in many roles because of my own engagement with the socialist movement since the 1960s.

In simple terms, George Fernandes was a *Karmayogi,* who exemplified the power and limits of parliamentary democracy in a post-colonial society. For many, his life journey resembled the hero of Albert Camus's *Myth of Sisyphus.* He was a man who was defined and recognized by his political action—not class, creed, ethnicity or party affiliation or successes and failures. He defied classical categorizations and contributed towards enlargement of the people's role and significance in parliamentary democracy in a newly independent nation with deep civilizational roots.

Four Phases of the Fascinating Public Life of George Fernandes

Chronologically, the eventful and illustrious life of George Fernandes may be divided into four phases: i. the formative years (1930-1967); ii. the giant killer (1967-1980); iii. the seeker of non-Congress alternatives (1980-2004); and iv. a lonely leader (2004-2019). Each phase deserves a detailed description. But we must be content with a summary view of each phase for our purpose of attempting to contextualize this man, who was among the makers of politics of non-Congressism through a) effective mass mobilizations, and b) several successful electoral competitions between 1964 and 2014.

George Fernandes was the eldest child of John Joseph Fernandes and Alice Martha. After completing the school education in his home-town Mangalore (Karnataka), he was sent by his parents to a seminary to be trained as a priest. But young George felt uncomfortable at the orthodox religious institute and soon left it to explore the future on his own. He found the life in Bombay more inviting where he was trained by socialist D'Mellow as a talented multi-lingual journalist-cum-trade unionist. He felt attracted to the ideas and activities of socialist thinker and leader Dr Ram Manohar Lohia. He became particularly close to socialist ideologue and parliamentarian Madhu Limaye by joining the Samyukta Socialist Party.

He attracted national attention by two acts of courage of conviction in the 1960s—first, he led a joint front of trade unions to organize the first ever 'Bombay Bandh'; secondly, entering the Lok Sabha in 1967 as a socialist from Bombay south by defeating the Congress stalwart and union minister S.K. Patil. He was called 'the giant killer' by the national media for it.

In the second phase from 1967 to 1980, George Fernandes, 'the Giant Killer', did not care for the compulsions of parliamentary politics. Lohia died in October 1967. George Fernandes, like most of the socialist parliamentarians, lost his parliamentary seat in the next general election of 1971 due to 'the Indira wave'. Soon Sarvodaya leader Jayaprakash Narayan attracted the non-Congress activists around his call for political reforms and anti-corruption policies. It led to a nation-wide surge for political change from Gujarat to Bihar and Uttar Pradesh. In the meanwhile, George Fernandes helped in bringing together the Indian socialists in a new Socialist Party under his presidentship. He became one of the top leaders of the Indian socialist movement and the Indian trade union movement. It was a period of political partnership with socialist stalwarts like Madhu Limaye, Rabi Ray, Ladli Mohan Nigam, J.H. Patel, Golap Barbora and Kapildeo Singh. Nearly 1 lakh political workers including J.P. and other non-Congress leaders were put behind the bars. Press censorship was imposed. Twenty-six organizations were banned. Congress (Indira), the Communist Party of India and Shiv Sena supported Government in it.

George Fernandes went 'underground' and soon became a symbol of national resistance against Indira Gandhi's Emergency Raj. He was arrested after several months and put on trial which became known as 'the Baroda dynamite case'. It created international protests. He became instrumental in the restoring of democracy as he was one of the very few mass leaders who were taken from prison to parliament after the elections of 1977 which ended the Emergency and the Indira Raj. As the Industries Minister of the first ever non-Congress government, he again attracted global attention by ordering the global corporate giants Coca Cola and IBM to close their activities and leave India. This period included the ten years of his married life to Leila Kabir (1971-'80) and being blessed by a son, Sean Fernandes.

The third phase (1980-2004) of the politics of George Fernandes was marked by accepting 'the compulsions of politics of non-

Congressism'. There was failure of the Janata Party government followed by the return of the Indira Gandhi-led Congress to power. The Congress continued in power between 1980 and 1999 with a short interruption between 1989 and 1992. Then came the era of 'Three 'Ms'—'Market, Mandal and Mandir'. It included the inauguration of 'new economic policies' which converged with the assertion of the Other Backward Classes through implementation of the Mandal Commission Report and the Hindutva forces mobilizing for destruction of the Babri Masjid and construction of a Sri Ram temple in Ayodhya.

George Fernandes opposed the new economic policies and supported the reservations for the OBCs. Of course, he did not agree with the politics of Hindu mobilization for temple-building. He persisted patiently for reconfiguration of non-Congress forces with a variety of political leaders from Charan Singh, Devi Lal, Chandra Shekhar, Biju Patanaik to V.P. Singh, Mufti Mohammed, Farooq Abdullah, Bal Thakare and L.K. Advani and contributed in setting up several non-Congress formations. It was not confined to electoral instruments. He also brought together anti-capitalist organizations, trade unions and civil society groups to resist the policies of neo-liberal globalization. He made several pragmatic adjustments to respond to the era of LPG—liberalization, privatization and globalization. His efforts yielded surprising results as there was again a non-Congress government of the National Democratic Alliance (NDA) from 1999 to 2004. This time George Fernandes was the convener of the NDA. Atal Bihari Vajpayee was the new Prime Minister who made him national Defence Minister.

The fourth and last phase of 2004 to 2019 may be termed as 'the period of lonely leader'. It was a period of resurgence of identity politics resulting in the rise of the Hindutva lobby within the BJP. On the other hand, the socialist space was increasingly occupied by a handful of leaders of the dominant castes in the non-Congress formations of UP, Bihar, Odisha, Maharashtra and Karnataka. His political instruments including the party organizations and trade unions were captured by ambitious 'followers' who found him irrelevant for caste-oriented regional vote-banks or ethnicized class politics.

He was 'defeated' in the contest for the presidentship of a party which was founded by him. It proved the irrelevance of his strategy to take forward his supporters beyond 'Mandalism' by connecting the call for 'social justice' with 'economic and political justice'. He was 'denied' a party ticket to contest the Lok Sabha election of 2014. He was replaced in the NDA by a gen-next socialist. He was already suffering from the advancement of neurological disorders. But he refused to give up. It was a tragedy to see him enter as a rebel candidate with a failing body and a handful of supporters. The Giant Killer of yesteryears was found to suffer a humiliating defeat from Muzaffarpur owing to his own fellow-travellers. Julius Caesar had one Brutus, but George Fernandes was confronted with too many.

Assessing George Fernandes as a socialist leader

Looking at these four phases spread over half a century, George Fernandes was found to be continuously struggling with the changing imperatives of Indian parliamentary politics. He entered the political space as a rebel with a socialist cause and concluded his journey as a pragmatic coalition leader of non-Congress political formations. He scored amazing successes in vote politics but there were increasing failures in his ideological orientation. For example, he began as a non-conformist of the Lohia-line of non-Congressism in 1963. But he ended up as a tireless campaigner of non-Congressism till the rise to power of the National Democratic Alliance in 1999 with the BJP-Shiv Sena nexus as the prime mover. Thus, he was a secular socialist who opted to be with Hindu-centric allies in order to continue with non-Congressism as well as survive the changing trends of parliamentary politics. Similarly, he was a socialist who was in a cabinet which welcomed global corporates by intensifying disinvestments and went further towards nuclearization of the nation. Therefore, it was not surprising that such a charismatic and courageous mass mobilizer ended up as a lonely leader at the end of six decades of amazing contributions and achievements.

Let us look at the political journey of George Fernandes in terms of seven major aspects, which may be considered relevant for a leader's evaluation:

Every leader has an ideological orientation and George Fernandes was second to none in being a democratic socialist in his personal life and public work. He was neither Marxist nor Gandhian. But he maintained a creative communication with all shades of Marxists and Gandhians.

A leader has an organizational background and George Fernandes created so many organizations. It is significant that there was uniqueness in many of the organizations promoted by him. He was a trans-national socialist who was a great supporter of all initiatives for freedom, justice, democracy and socialism within the country and every part of the world. It made him very respected among the Tibetans, the Nepalese, the Bhutanese, the Sri Lankans, the Bangladeshis, the Iranians, the South Africans, the Blacks and the European Greens.

There is a third dimension around the nature of activism. He was quite a unique combination of responsible activist and exemplary parliamentarian. Most of the socialists lose after two to three terms because of anti-incumbency and a variety of other factors. But the way he made himself acceptable to a wide range of voters in south Mumbai, Muzaffarpur, Banka and Nalanda was amazing. He was the most charismatic leader in the Lohia tradition and that made him acceptable to all shades of social activists. This appeal among the activists was his basic political capital—his charisma emerging from his courage, his courage growing out of his conviction and his conviction rooted in the legacy of the Indian socialist movement.

The fourth thing for any leader is the social roots and that is the most amazing part in the case of George Fernandes. The social roots of George Fernandes were in one way his asset and in another way, his handicap. He did not belong to the dominant region or religion or the dominant castes or the dominant class. Still he had a larger-than-life personality where everybody could feel included and wanted.

Every leader is assessed with the help of an account of her/his successes. The success of George Fernandes is memorable on several counts. First, he was the last national leader of the socialists. He knew eight languages and was equally comfortable in Kashmir and Kerala. He was both interested in and accessible for Gujarat and Manipur. This was his most memorable contribution to the socialist movement and Indian democracy. He also created a new network for bridging the gap between the generation of Narendra Dev-Lohia-Jayaprakash and the generation after George Fernandes through continuous communication and constant activities. Finally, he strengthened the class base of the socialist movement through institutional innovations and organizational investment. He developed complementarity between the class organizations and electoral parties. He was an iconic trade unionist and effective parliamentarian at the same time.

How did he relate to his colleagues and followers? Was he a capacity enhancer who nurtured a new set of leaders? His followers were very passionate in their love for the leader but equally argumentative with their own leader. He cultivated the art of dialogue and discussion among his co-workers through pages of his periodicals—*Other Side* (English) and *Pratipaksh* (Hindi). He created spaces for his younger colleagues and encouraged them to adopt new initiatives. He was an inspiring leader who taught many younger men and women all over the country to lead movements and organizations.

Was he dogmatic or open-minded? George Fernandes was always eager to interact with activists of other ideological traditions and political movements. He did pay attention to the details of a given situation, but he never insisted on following a conventional approach. It made him an ever-evolving leader with fresh insights and ideas.

There were four limitations of George Fernandes and his times:

The first limitation was the persistence of the ideological and political hegemony of the Congress Party and its near absolute rule till 1977. When George Fernandes entered the political life of India in the early 1960s, the Indian political life was commanded and guided by the charismatic superhero called Jawaharlal Nehru. But George Fernandes, the rebel, sided with one of the most marginal forces of the time, Dr Ram Manohar Lohia and his handful of socialist followers.

Second, he was over-committed to the politics of non-Congressism. Originally, it was a tactic, not even a strategy. But the atrocities of the Emergency Raj transformed it into an article of faith. After the brutalizing experiences of the Emergency, George Fernandes became totally convinced that there was nothing good or positive left in the Congress due to the suffocating control of Indira Gandhi and her coterie.

Third, the Indian Communists were always hostile to him as he had elementary differences with the Marxist paradigm of socialism. It is another matter that it did not make him anti-Communist. He continued sincere efforts of dialogue and cooperation with a wide spectrum of Marxists and Maoists in his initiatives of building non-Congress formations for collective action. He believed that they had a passion for the well-being of the marginalized masses which is unmatchable. He had a similar orientation about the so-called 'separatists' in Kashmir, Punjab, and the North-East.

Finally, the fetish of continuing to maintain a parliamentary identity was also a serious limitation in the later part of the political life of a matchless socialist leader like George Fernandes. The power of parliament for a post-colonial democracy was unfathomable. It was true that Gandhi was not impressed and Jayaprakash never contested for it. But the desire to be active in parliament was quite intoxicating for all Indian democrats, including the Lohia socialists till the1980s. Later, the institution of parliament got much more demystified as people became aware of how these elections were won. It was increasingly related to money power than people's power. It began to be asked: socialism for entering parliament or becoming a member of parliament for strengthening socialism? That is the dilemma which was confronted by the generation of George Fernandes in the 1990s. It is perplexing that he decided to remain an 'insider' with the help of a non-Congress coalition; whereas his two other closest colleagues Madhu Limaye and Rabi Ray walked away from the parliamentary game to remain closer to the dynamics of building a socialist India.

Fighter Against Tyranny

Farooq Abdullah

Democracy cannot progress unless we are prepared to share and understand each other. We may differ, but we differ to agree on many of the things that might be good for the people. George was one of those persons who was absolutely simple. He dressed simply, walked simply and talked simply. He was a people's man. He came from the bottom. Even when he rose to the highest seat, he never forgot the earth on which he was walking or the people he knew. There was no guard in his house even when he was the Defence Minister. Open door! You could walk in. You could walk into any room, even his bedroom. Today, they do not allow you to even get near the minister's door.

There are some things I would like to tell you about him. As the Defence Minister, he wanted to meet terrorist groups in Kashmir to find out what was ailing them, why they had taken to a revolt against the nation. What was the reason? He came to my house and said, "I have to go and meet these people." I said, "George, you are the Defence Minister. Now, how the hell can I tell you that without security you will go and if you are shot dead, who am I going to answer to? Because nobody is going to trust me that you forced me to allow you to do this." He had a very loyal personal secretary. I have forgotten his name. I tried to convince him but George remained unconvinced. So there was an editor of one of the newspapers who had arranged a meeting with some of these people and I said, "O God, I hope he comes back safely." At ten o' clock in the night, alone in the car, the Defence Minister of India travels with an editor of a newspaper to meet these people. He returns at two o' clock, convinced that he has told them that we mean well and that we will look into their problems. That was

George. I wish the present Defence Minister would go. I do not think so.

The second incident was in a remote area of Deodar. A Colonel who was loved by the people was shot by a terrorist. The Army unit of that area burnt the entire village and as the Chief Minister I visited that area. It was a very difficult area. We had to land the helicopter on the top of a mountain on a patch so small that if you were not on it you would be miles down in the ravine. I walked to that village and I saw their plight. They had nothing to do with it. I rang George. I said, "I want you to come. I want you to see what has happened. We do not want to lose people." George came and brought the Northern Commander with him and my chopper had landed at that place. We collected the people. The Defence Minister of India apologized to those people. They were ordinary people, absolutely ordinary people and I wonder whether they had even food. He told them, "We made a mistake. We apologize." He made the General apologize and said, "Within twenty-four hours your supplies will be there and your new homes will start being constructed." That was George.

The third incident. You know we jam radios. There was an absolutely revolting radio from the PoK—Pakistan Occupied Kashmir—that used to have propaganda which was so vicious that the Government of India decided to ban this, jam this channel, so that you will not be able to get anything from there. We were sitting in my sitting room and he said, "Farooq, we have jammed this station." I said, "Really, you have jammed this station?" I brought my transistor and put that channel on. That channel was vomiting whatever it could against India. I said, "George, here is the channel." He said, "Really?" It didn't take him much time to ring every single person and say, "You were fooling the nation. The channel is still there." And let me tell you, he was human. Once you sit on the chair you lose that touch. You become God. Overnight you think you are the only one and there is no one more powerful and stronger than you. This was the man who, even sitting on that chair was humble. Now, that you will never see. I have not seen it in many of these leaders except one man whose name was Vajpayee. He was the only man from the RSS, Jana Sangh, who realized that this nation belongs to all of us, and that unless we all progress, this nation can never progress. I mean, look at the man. We are fighting in the state of Jammu and Kashmir against the terrorism from Pakistan, yet, he crosses the border and stands where Pakistan was announced, in Lahore, *Nishane-Pakistan* and stands and says, "I, Prime Minister of India representing 1.2 billion people, am here to tell you that we accept Pakistan as a country. We want you to be strong and want you to be friends with us." Where are those leaders today? Do you see George anywhere? What do you see today? Lies being dished out by the channels who are paid to do so. Those of us who believe in God, there are many who do not believe in God any more now, wonder sometimes when this power is going to strike these people who are destroying the very values of humanity. What do you see around? If you say anything which they will not accept, you are anti-national, you are pro-Pakistan. When my state joined the Union of India, it was not the power of the gun that you have or the Air Force or the Navy. It joined because there was this man wearing a *dhoti,* called Gandhi who preached and gave his life for an understanding of humanity. Today we don't see Gandhis. We see people who are hungry for power and prepared to do everything for it, even kill people. Soldiers die every day in my state. There is not a day—how many times has any minister from the Central Government gone to their families or had a ceremony for them? Even yesterday three or four of my CRPF *jawans* were shot dead. Does anybody cry about that? What has happened to us? What has happened to Indians? Where is our soul? Do we have a soul?

I wish George were alive. He fought against the Emergency, against tyranny. He didn't care whether he would die in prison or be hanged. But he fought for a cause that that was wrong, that we are free people. We are not slaves any more. We are not British slaves but we have become slaves in our own nation. We have given up and accept whatever is being told us is absolutely right. We need to make corrections if we want to save the nation. I am a Muslim. I don't tell a Christian or a Hindu or a Sikh how he should live, how he should pray, what he should do, what he should eat. It is his job. It is not my job. But today we are told you can eat this, you can't eat this, you can't do this, you have to do this. To my dying day I am not going to accept it. I was born a captive of the

British. I am not going to live to my grave as a slave.

If you really want to remember George then remember what he fought for. You know, when 1984 happened, I was in a small hotel in Connaught Place. That was a Sikh's hotel. They came to burn it and those people who were there said, "Look, we are Hindus. What are you burning?" How we saved our lives God only knows. Then I realized that we are still animals. Even if we are educated, we are still animals. We have no respect for human beings. Then when I walked with those leaders to Punjabi Bagh and the other places and when I was asked by Gujral Sahab, "Could you please come and take out this great soldier from Bhogal, the very General who saved Bangladesh from Pakistan's occupation?", I said, "Sir, I'll come, but tell the General to wear the uniform." I picked up Gujral Sahab from his house and Bhogal is near Friends Colony or what you call Maharani Bagh. From there, I drove and this General had four soldiers to protect him, who were Gurkhas. There were houses burning on the right side, the Mercedes, the cars, the people and suddenly this General walks out wearing a suit. I made him sit. I said, "Sir, please sit down." I said, "Sir, I had requested you to put this uniform on." He said, "Farooq, that uniform today has a big patch and I couldn't wear it because of what hatred has been generated in this nation." I told him, "Where do I take you, Sir?" Gujral said, "Drop me first at my house." I asked him, "Where do I take you?" He said, "I want to go to the Army Command because I want to know if it takes two days for the Army to move from Meerut." That's where the garrison was. So I dropped him and said, "Sir, do I take you back?" He said, "No."

What is this nation going through? You lynch a Muslim just because he is carrying the cows. You kill a Police Officer who is protecting people and nobody bats an eye. Where are we going? What is our direction? On one hand you say that Kashmir is an integral part of India, on the other, the stupid governor of one of the states of this nation says, "Don't go to Kashmir. Don't go to Amarnath Yatra and don't buy any food that is Kashmiri." Then why are we Indians? Why don't you say goodbye to us? We will find our way. If this is the way that you want to treat us then why the hell should we stay with you? What is the compulsion for us to stay with you? If you do not want us, well goodbye. Remember, in the Quran, "I am the one who feeds you and the day I want to stop feeding you, you will not get it." And I give you an example. This Prophet told God once, Moses told Him, "How are we going to survive?" He said, because Moses used to go to God and talk to Him there. He said, "Moses, go down. Break that stone. You will get your answer." He broke the stone and there was a small ant or insect alive in the middle of the stone. The voice of God came and said, "Have you got your answer?" He bowed down and said, "O Lord, I was wrong." It is this what we want from you. We do not want your wealth. We don't want your great palaces. We want your love and understanding. Give us that love. Understand our hurts. There must be something wrong somewhere that I may have done it. Can't we find a way out? Can't we sit down together and say, "Well this is one nation. Let's find what is ailing you and try to find a solution to the problem. How do I tell my young children that we are part of this nation when they see people being lynched just because they are Muslims? You know, when 1984 happened, I went to a house and Sikhs were collected there, and this gentleman told me, "Farooq, today we realized why Muslims live in ghettos. It is because they can protect themselves." We still haven't taken that hatred out of ourselves. That we are all one. I mean, as a doctor, if you have a pain in your stomach is there a different medicine for a Hindu, for a Sikh, for a Christian, for a Buddhist, because you are different religions? It is one medicine. How are we being divided? Why are we being divided? With what thought? And then look at the political parties. They cannot get together. Each one thinks that it is mightier than the other. I wonder after the election what they will think.

And how we fool people. So many thousand crores for this, so many thousand crores for that, where are those thousands of crores? We were promised eighty thousand crores. Out of that, the last Chief Minister said that we got only ten thousand crores. Where is the seventy thousand crores? What do I tell people? They say, "Leader *chor hai*." Imagine, forty thousand crores is given to the Members of Parliament for local development. Forty thousand crores! Five hundred crores every year a Member of Parliament gets for attending to local work. Do you know that thirty per cent of that money is consumed by the officers? And our Prime

Minister says, "I am going to eliminate corruption." I wanted to build a small hospital in Jammu in an area where I live so that people who are very poor can be treated there. If a snake bite takes place, before he gets to the hospital he'll die, so they can treat them in the hospital, or if some small illnesses take place. If there is a major issue, a woman is pregnant and the baby is twisted around and cannot be delivered and has to be taken immediately to the hospital, we have kept an ambulance. I kept one crore, many years ago. The man in charge came to me and said, "Please take this money back." I said, "Why? Why are you asking me to take this money back?" He said, "Because the officers are telling me that ten lakhs are for you, twenty lakhs for us officers and ten lakhs for the builder. Sir, sixty lakhs will be left. What will we build?" Has anybody thought? Have any of you considered what is happening to this money? No one! As if *hum logon ne afeem kha lee hai*, that we are so intoxicated with something that it doesn't matter whether the river flows this way or another way or whether the country goes to hell or to heaven, it doesn't make a difference. I think the time has come for this nation to wake up and unless you wake up the nation cannot wake up. In the elections we meet here, discuss matters here. How much of a difference does it make to the people? How much? We had a surgical strike. Oh wonderful! We shot one of their planes and you say, "Where is the proof of the plane that you shot?" Now where is the proof that you say, Amit Shah says that three hundred people died? Where is the proof of those three hundred? And if you ask you are anti-national, you are against the country.

The time has come when you should ask questions, when you should say, "Where are we going? What direction are we taking?"This is not the India that I knew as a child. I wish that India returns. I don't know whether it will return. In the memory of George, a fighter—a fighter for truth who accepted mistakes boldly. The first man who had the courage to say in Parliament that in Nehru's own writing there is no sensitive place that should be given to a Muslim. The first man in the Parliament of India and the only bold man who said that the danger is from China. Pakistan is no danger, let me tell you. Pakistan does not make a difference. The Chinese don't want to show us that they are our enemies. So they are using the back channel through them to pinprick us. That was George. Can you imagine that as Defence Minister he goes to America, and he was stripped? When I told Vajpayeeji that I had to go to America but I did not want to be stripped like he was, he said, "Then don't go to America." I went and can you imagine, when I came to New York it was fine because the Indian Embassy people arrived and they collected me, very well. I had to go with eight doctors of Indian origin to play golf and see Las Vegas. All my friends are sitting in the plane and I am waiting near the desk and say, "Why the hell am I not going? What is the problem?" So I told this lady who was at the desk, I said, "What is wrong? I am sitting here. My plane must have left." She got worried because we people have a very high tone when we speak. Even my wife sometimes says, "Are you quarrelling?" I say, "No, no, this is my way of speaking." Then I have to apologize several times. So, this officer appears from inside. He says, "Sir, we are very sorry. Your passport has a visa for Iraq." I said, "Yes, India is a friend of all countries. What is wrong with Iraq? We are not Americans. We are Indians." He said, "That is all, Sir." I gave him whatever I could. I couldn't care a shit for America. I said, "Now my plane must have gone." He said, "No, Sir, we have held the plane back." And do you know like Jesus Christ I was like this. I said, "The next time I come to America I will wear a banana leaf in front and leave the back side without any cover." Now when I got into the plane, you wouldn't believe, everyone of them was looking at me thinking, "Who the hell is this who has held this plane for one hour?" I did not dare to go to the bathroom afterwards because I thought if I went to the bathroom, they would say, "This fellow is going to take this plane somewhere else." This is what I saw when the 1984 events took place. We Muslims were always searched, our caps were taken off and suddenly I saw Sardarjis going through the same process. The minute a Sardarji got up, everybody shivered *ki ab yeh kya Pakistan jayega ya kidhar jayega*? I used to be happy seated there thinking how they had to deal with the same issue we had to deal with. That was the situation.

This nation has gone through tragedies, unnecessary tragedies. If you want to build a temple, who is stopping you from building the temple? I will tell you a story which is true. I was studying medicine in Jaipur and used to come with Suresh, a doctor friend of mine to his house in Delhi. Those days Delhi was not as it is today. It was a small, peaceful town with hardly any cars. They used to live in Daryaganj where they had migrated from Pakistan. The father had died. My friend was from Multan and had a very affectionate mother, God bless her, she was a short woman. There used to be a lot of talk about Ram, Ram, Ram, about doing this to Ram and doing that to Ram. While I was sitting and having my meal, his poor mother was cooking chapattis for us. She asked me, "*Beta*, what is all this about Ram?" I said, "*Ma*, I am not a Hindu, I do not know." She told me that Ram is universal Ram (*vishwa ka Ram*). This was the old lady telling me that he is not only an Indian Ram and that it was mentioned in their scriptures that Ram is universal. So he is your Ram whether you accept it or not. He is also your Ram. Now this has stuck. Years after, God bless that fellow's soul also, who used to be one of the great fighters for Ram Mandir and things like this. One day there was an event going on in Himachal Bhawan and I was also on the stage. While they were saying all these things, I remembered his mother telling me this years ago and so I said to him, "Is Ram only your Ram?" So, this fellow got surprised. He asked, "What do you mean?" I replied, "I think this old lady told me that in your scriptures it is written that he is a universal Ram. He is Ram for Christians, Muslims, for the English, Russians, anybody who wants to know him, he is their Ram." He was dumbstruck. What should he say? I said, "If he is only your Ram then you keep him, but if he is *vishwa ka Ram* then you should accept that I also accept him."

This is what we have created. We have created hatred within each other without understanding the basics of it. Jesus was not only Christians' Jesus. When he came, he came for all. He did not come only for the Christians. Christians may have owned him but he never came only for Christians. He is as much our prophet as theirs, but we don't say he is only mine. For instance, One God is a Universal God, all these universes, Rab-ul-alamin, the universe, not Rab-ul-Muslamin, that is mine only, or the prophet, peace be on his soul, Rehmat-ul-allah-amin, he brings prosperity and love for all. Why have we created divisions in ourselves? What for? It is because our political and religious leaders wanted to divide us for their own good, not for the good of the people. Had our religious leaders and our political leaders given that path up and said, "No, God is the Creator for all of us."

I went to Baku during the Russian time when there was the USSR and they took me to this cave. Now what did I see in this cave? Fire coming out, a *trishul* there brought by some saints who had travelled to those lands and this man was telling me that Guru Nanak came there. There is a story which I was told. When Guru Nanak travelled to Mecca and he was lying with his feet towards the mosque that we go round. The religious people who managed to ensure that people don't do anything wrong, came to him, "What are you doing? Your feet are towards Kabah. What are you doing this for?" He said, '*Achchha,* I am sorry, please can you move them?" He moved the feet and he sees Kabah move in the direction of his feet, whichever direction he moved. This man went up and said, "God's man, I am sorry." In this *kalyug* these people have disappeared. We have devils around, no saints are left. When will such a saint come who will save this nation, you and us so that we can live in harmony and in love for each other? We need that love for each other. Let us pray to God that we see that India return where we love each other, give everything for each other, for you will take nothing, you have come with nothing and you will take nothing. If you remember that then your desire for peace will increase. Let us hope this desire for peace will increase in those leaders who today spread nothing but venom against each other.

God bless George, his soul. God bless his family. God bless you, his friends. I never saw him once he was away. It was difficult to get to him, but he was always here. I remember, whenever I was pained how I used to go to him and sit down with him. More than you who are his blood brothers, was his affection and love for me. That I can never forget. He died too early like all good people go. Let us hope this nation will produce another guide who will steer this nation to prosperity and humanity. This is how I feel. I see my nation die. It hurts me that when I go down and meet these friends there, what will I tell them as to what direction we have led ourselves. Pray. There is no power greater than God's power. Pray to Him and pray for this nation while you pray for yourself, to lead us towards a better India, the India that will shine more than the stars and the sun because it will be a nation of peace, harmony and understanding for the whole world.

George, thank you. I am thankful to God that I was able to come. Jaya had invited me to Bombay. I couldn't go because the situation in Kashmir was desperately bad. We are still going through terrible turmoil. We are not sure what's going to happen. Our young have gone completely astray. How we will pull them back I do not know. I really don't know because it is a pathetic situation. I mean, look at Nehru, he could jump into a crowd of lakhs where Farooq Abdullah has to take gunmen to walk on the street. You wouldn't believe, my wife says to me, "What the hell are we living in?" She goes for six months to England and she feels free there. She says, "Is this what India is?" What do I tell her? She cannot go to a shop unless she has a bullet proof vehicle and has people around her. Pray for us. Pray for the people of the state that God gets them out of this turmoil and pray that our neighbour realizes that they are not going to win and will never be able to take any territory. They know it fully well. Vajpayee asked me before he went across the border, "Farooq, what do I do?" I said, "Sir, when you go across tell them, "Keep that. We keep this." We straighten the line. We make the line easy for people to come and go so that there is no hatred between people." And God bless his soul, he did go and told Nawaz Sharif exactly the same thing. When he came back, he called me and said, "Farooq exactly the same words I told them and Nawaz Sharif said that this is the only solution but today to convince the Army would be difficult."

This will be the solution for the state of Jammu and Kashmir. But let us hope it will be a happy one, that we love each other and destroy the fibres of hatred.

Here let me say how did I know George Mathew. Yes, it was through George Fernandes. We wanted to have Panchayati Raj in Jammu and Kashmir, the basic government so that our people would be empowered. That is how I got to know George Mathew. I sent three of my ministers to Karnataka, who had really started Panchayat Raj. Then, when we compiled the document of Panchayat Raj, we consulted George Mathew. He was actually the mastermind of correcting us and making Panchayat Raj really workable. But unfortunately, we politicians sometimes do not agree on some issues, and one such issue we did not agree was: whether the Chairman of the Panchayat in the last year of the Panchayat Raj should be elected or if he/she should be selected. The document was for the chairman to be elected. There should be no selection of the gentleman or the lady. But my MLAs were not very happy. Their point was: what they would do if the fellow is also elected and that their interest would be harmed, not realizing that their work and the Panchayat President/Chairman's work are different. Somehow, we are so power-hungry that once we sit on the chair we never want to leave it and we do not want to share it with anybody. That is the unfortunate situation about our politics which is destroying this nation. So, we had to give in. I can assure George Mathew that if God gives us power again to return, the first thing that we are going to do is that the local governments will have elected chairpersons.

God bless this nation. God bless George Fernandes wherever he is...

George the Democrat

Michael B. Fernandes

George's democratic outlook is a subject of discussion. I want to give an example of that, at the trade union movement level. In the 1990's there was a National Executive Committee meeting of the HMKP (Hind Mazdoor Kisan Panchayat). And eight people were sitting on one side. George, naturally as the President, was there. I was there as a Vice-President, and there were six others. Some complications arose in the discussions and then I had to bring to the notice of the meeting saying: "Look, we are eight of us here, and we are in eight different parties. All of us are in politics but no two, not even him (George) and me, are in the same party". George was in Samata and I was in JD(U). I am mentioning this only to confirm, with a solid example of this kind, that he was really very democratic.

Between me and George, the relationship was without any kind of friction, at any time. From the time he left Mangalore till he died we have not clashed. As small boys, of course, we fought and all that. As we grew up we have helped each other, but have also been ourselves—each one by himself. I contested for the Bangalore City Council election in 1970 as an Independent and won. Subsequently in 1977, I was in the Janata Party; became an MLA and then an MLC also, but George never dictated to me "You do this or that" or be in his party, etc.

I should clear one thing about George, of what is being said about him, that he joined the seminary to become a priest at the instance and under the pressure of our parents, because it was then a tradition in Mangalore for families to give a priest, or a nun, to the Catholic Church. It was not George's idea initially to become a priest. He did so to avoid our father's pressure on him to join college and then become a lawyer, which he did not want to do. So, as an escape route, he decided to become a priest.

In many newspaper articles, George is said to have moved to Mumbai (then Bombay) in search of a job, but since he did not get one he had to sleep on the footpaths. That is not the case. When George left the seminary and came back to Mangalore, he joined the Socialist movement there by enrolling himself in the Socialist Party. At that time he, along with Placid D'Mello, leader of dock workers' union, who was externed from Bombay Presidency by the government, conducted labour strikes against the hotel owners and a transport company in Mangalore. Both the strikes failed, but the hotel workers collected some money from their own resources, and gave it to George to go to Bombay, become a lawyer and then return and help them. That is the way George went to Bombay and the rest is history. Therefore to say that George went to Bombay in search of a job is absolutely incorrect.

After D'Mello returned to Bombay, George joined the dock workers' union. But when D'Mello was away again for a while, there was some kind of misunderstanding among some union leaders and George was perhaps seen as an outsider. So he went out and worked for just one month and a half for *The Times of India* as a proof reader and soon thereafter went back to the dock workers' union. His prominence as a labour leader from then onwards, and particularly after earning the "George the Giant Killer" title by winning the Lok Sabha seat from Bombay South in 1967, did not create any sign of self-aggrandizement in him, or for that matter, in our entire family too—not in George, not in his brothers and not in his parents. George and Paul were both in the trade union movement, and then I too joined the labour movement and became a trade union functionary in 1961.

Lawrence was not a trade union functionary, but a member being a worker. When it came to the Emergency (in 1975) the three of us were in prison—George, Lawrence and myself. And we have done whatever we have done, only for the benefit of people at large.

With this I stop talking about George in the past tense. As for the future tense, we have to carry forward his legacy. For me, two things stand out very prominently: one is the cooperative bank that he started. Now I have assumed George's work by becoming the President of the HMKP. My efforts will be to carry that cooperative bank idea all over the country. It is unfortunate that in his time, it was not carried out elsewhere; an attempt was made on one occasion but it failed for some reason. And now I think, in the process of carrying George's legacy forward, we need to do something concrete: he has left behind a cooperative bank for the people and it will be my effort to take that movement forward. I am sure that we will succeed in that.

The other thing I would like to do is to involve the HMKP in raising funds for the "George Fernandes Chair on Labouring and Marginalized Peoples" at the Institute of Social Sciences. For this purpose, I would certainly make it an agenda for the HMKP and hope that I will be able to do something for it.

George My Brother

Paul B.R. Fernandes

January 29, 2019 was the worst day in my life. It was a very bad day in Toronto in terms of weather, with heavy snow and ice. I was stuck in traffic for several hours in the night. On that night I got a call from my brother Michael in India about George's passing away.

My own relationship in the family has been very close, but my relationship with our eldest in the family, George, was very special and dear.

I remember when our father passed away in 1983, I came home for the funeral. When George saw me, he embraced me. Then I said to myself: "Here is my new father". That's the way he considered me in our family.

I do not know anyone who has done as much as George had done in India for the poor and the working class. He had tremendous commitment to the unorganized workers. He founded the Bombay Labour Union in 1963 because there were a number of small factories where the workers could not form trade unions. George's mission was to empower the small factory workers, the hotel workers, the taximen, the Bombay State Transport workers, the Dock workers as well as those working in the Indian Railways. When there was an all-India indefinite strike in 1963, to express solidarity with the strikers, there was a one-day sympathy strike called by several unions including the LIC union of which I was the general secretary of the Western Zone. On that day, late in the evening when I went home there were many of my friends waiting for me. They looked very depressed and told me that George was beaten up on the railway tracks at the Dadar Railway Station and he was being held in the Arthur Road Jail. I immediately got in touch with the Chief Minister's office and told the secretary that I wanted to see George. But I was only told that he was in the Arthur Road Jail. I said again that I would like to go there and see him. The reply was: "No, you can't. You'll have to get the permission from the Chief Minister." Then I went to see the Chief Minister at his Malabar Hill official residence and he asked his secretary to give me a letter addressed to the jail authorities which enabled me to go and see George. He had been beaten up very badly and was in great pain. His slogan those days was: "Bombay bandh" and then finally it became "Bharat bandh". As you all know, he was a great organizer of trade unions and organizer of strikes. George was an outstanding labour leader both nationally and internationally.

I moved to Canada in 1966. The first time that George came to Canada was in 1969 and we were at Queen's Park, the Ontario Provincial Legislature. There we had a luncheon meeting with the leader of the New Democratic Party, which was known as Canada's Socialist Party. They don't use the term socialist at all. We had lunch with the leader of NDP and then we were there for the question period at the legislature. Later in the evening, when we were on our way home, at Yonge and Bloor subway station George asked me: "Paul, what are you doing here?" I felt George was disappointed with me. It was because, he had seen me in Bombay being very active. When I left India, I was the general secretary of the All India Life Insurance Employees' Association (AILIEA). He had seen me always in action, especially when I was responsible for organizing a hunger strike. That was in 1963 which was a day I will never forget. He let me down by what he said. At the Sundaribai Hall Rally after a two-day hunger strike we had several speakers—politicians and trade unionists. The national president of the AILIEA Rui Menezes welcomed everybody and I was the first speaker. I addressed all the issues involved for about twenty minutes or so. After that George was the third speaker and as he started speaking in Hindi, within the first five minutes he said *"humara bhai ne jo kaha hai, Paul humara chhota bhai hai"* and that created many problems for me. In my union, barring my very close associates and personal friends, people didn't know that George was my brother. I never went around saying that George Fernandes was my brother. So, the next day when I went to my regular Life Insurance Corporation office in Santa Cruz, I had a number of people who came to me and asked if George Fernandes was my brother. I said "yes." "Real brother?" I said "yes". "So, what does it mean? Am I going to get more respect now?" So that was one problem he created for me. A number of people were ready to hit me actually, you know, "you never told me".

So, George had seen me in action in Bombay for many years. He was the only one in the family who did not want me to leave India. He wanted me to be involved in politics and the labour movement in India. That evening in Toronto at the subway station he said, "Paul, what are you doing here?" It was because I was not actively involved in activities as in Bombay. Of course, I had started some work but then as time went by he realized I was doing a lot more than what he expected. I was Vice-President of the Toronto & District Liberal Association, I was the Chairman of the Catholic School Board, Toronto. That was the largest School Board in the country at that time. I was a Trustee for six years, and served on boards of many organizations including the Toronto East General Hospital and the North York Community Credit Union. I was involved in fundraising for many charitable organizations, the Rotary Club, the Knights of Columbus, much involved with the Vietnamese Refugees in the nineteen eighties, and helping people in many areas including arranging jobs. When George came to know about my extensive involvement in many organizations, he asked me: "Paul, where do you find the time to do all that you are doing? You also have to earn to look after your family?"

George had met several people in Toronto and elsewhere in Canada, Ottawa, Hamilton, Peterborough, numerous places where I had taken him and many people were quite impressed and learnt quite a lot from him in terms of community work and commitment to society.

George used to come to Toronto quite often and spend a lot of time travelling.

In 1985, he came twice to Canada. Before his second visit, he was in Stockholm. From there, he called me and said "Paul, send me a London-Toronto return ticket and make an appointment with the lawyer who was involved in the Watergate issue." So, I sent him a ticket immediately. He arrived the next day. With George, on that trip, I think I probably drove over eight thousand kilometres going to Fairfax, Virginia, Washington, New York, Buffalo, then several cities in Canada including Ottawa.

One day in 2004 when George returned to Delhi from Patna after midnight, he called me at 2.00 a.m. and said "Paul, I just returned from Patna. There are heavy floods there which have caused heavy damage. What can you do for us?", I asked: "When can you come here?" He replied: "Anytime." The following month I organized a fundraising dinner and the proceeds went to *Bihar Viklang Kalyan Parishad* (BVKP} in George's Parliamentary constituency.

My second oldest brother, Lawrence, passed away in November 2005, and after his funeral, we five brothers were sitting and discussing about things to do. Noticing that he was struggling to adjust his hearing aid, I figured out that his health had deteriorated. While returning to Toronto, I passed through New Delhi when I asked him: "When was the last time you had a complete medical check up?" He replied: "One year seven months ago". I said that he should go for a complete checkup. His reply was "Where will I find four days for that?" Just then Nitish Kumar arrived from Patna to address a joint press conference with George pertaining to the election results in Bihar. During the press conference, Nitish Kumar had to take control because George was not able to respond to questions from the Press. When we were returning home, Anil Hegde, George's personal assistant told me that several reporters asked him: "Is George Sahab not well?"So, it is obvious that his health problems had started much earlier.

In 2007, when George and his friend, Hans Janitschek, former Secretary General of Socialist International were in Toronto, I once again organized a fundraising dinner for BVKP. But at that time he was not the same George. His health and memory had much declined. George was in Toronto for over three weeks and had a complete medical check-up. The Doctors told me that he had Alzheimer's.

Then on January 17, 2008 when a major event to honour George was organized in Bangalore, with the Dalai Lama as the chief guest, it was a memorable occasion. Hans and I wrote a three-minute speech for George which he was unable to read. He kept declining fast.

So, he has set a tremendous and a great example for the labour leaders and politicians of today and tomorrow. I hope that many will emulate the example set by George.

George the Eternal Rebel

Neerja Chowdhury

If one were to sum up George Fernandes's contribution to the Indian story, it was to deepen democracy in the country.

He fought for the rights of the working class in the first decades of his public life. Taximen of Mumbai and railwaymen all over the country loved him and looked upto him as their leader.

In 1974, he had disrupted the entire railway network with his successful all-India strike. The 1.7 million railway workers he had mobilized, over rights denied to them, brought the country to a grinding halt. The strike lasted 20 days, and dealt a body blow to the incumbent Congress government. It was seen as a milestone in the decline of the Congress which had won India its independence and had till then ruled the country for almost three decades.

What is more, it was only three years earlier, the then Prime Minister Indira Gandhi, at the peak of her popularity for having helped create the new nation of Bangladesh, was being hailed as Goddess "Durga".

Fernandes will also be remembered for his fight for democratic freedoms, endangered during the 1975-77 Emergency imposed by Indira Gandhi, when she threw opposition leaders in jail and enforced censorship of the press. He opposed the Emergency, first by going underground and defying arrest for a whole year. Unlike other political leaders who were detained on the night of June 25, 1975, George had got wind of the impending arrests and managed to give a slip to the police looking for him.

I was working at the time for *Himmat* Magazine, a Mumbai-based weekly opposing censorship. We would wait for those thrilling stories of how Fernandes, on the run, had stayed in a particular place for a few hours and then managed a getaway

L to R: Michael Fernandes, Farooq Abdullah, George Mathew, Jaya Jaitly and Paul Fernandes

L to R: Ash Narain Roy, Kalon Karma Yeshi, George Mathew, Dick Gupwell, and G.M. Patil

A Section of Audience

Suresh Prabhu

Sumit Chakravartty

K. C. Tyagi

Ravi Nair

Neerja Choudhary

Anand Kumar

Dolma Gyari

before the police got wind of his whereabouts. Some of us were helping the local socialists in Mumbai to put together underground leaflets in 1976, with news that could not be published because of censorship, and we would get the latest news through the informal grapevine.

In June 1976, however, he was betrayed, and arrested. During the Emergency, Fernandes was also charged in what came to be known as the Baroda Dynamite case.

In jail, and this was the buzz at the time, a bright light was shone at him constantly to prevent him from sleeping. Then came the day, when he was brought to court in chains, and in complete defiance of the might of the Indian state, he vowed to fight against Indira Gandhi's dictatorship.

That photograph of a chained Fernandes is now an indelible part of India's political history. So is his fight, from prison, in the 1977 general election, from Muzaffarpur in Bihar on a Janata Party ticket. He won it handsomely.

My first meeting with George Fernandes was some time in the late 1960s. Rajmohan Gandhi had invited Fernandes to meet a group of us in Mumbai. Most of us were in our teens then, in college or just out of it, and we had come to Mumbai for a programme. He was being hailed as a "giant killer" who had just defeated the Congress heavyweight S.K. Patil in the 1967 elections.

He spoke to us about India, about his work with the trade unions, his early start as a priest, which his parents wanted him to be. He oozed charm, energy, drive, ready to take on the powerful and change the lot of the poor and the deprived.

Then he offered to drive us around Mumbai—some of us had come to the metropolis for the first time—in his car. It was a black one (I do not recall its make) but I remember several of us managed to squeeze in at the back as we went around the city. He took us to his office (somewhere near Charni Road) and told us how he had slept on the bench there on many nights.

The third facet of his role as a democrat lay in helping to build an alternative to the Congress, then a powerful force in Indian politics, in power nationally and in states. He knew the import of a strong opposition, so essential for the survival of a democratic polity. George supported political groups opposed to the Congress, and often helped to bring them together on a common platform. Mentored by the original author of anti-Congressism in the country, Ram Manohar Lohia, his baptism had taken place early.

In 1967 itself, he had taken on Congress strongman S.K. Patil in his own den in Mumbai. That year the Samyukta Vidhayak Dal coalition governments (comprising the Bharatiya Kranti Dal, the Samyukta Socialist Party, the Praja Socialist Party and the Jana Sangh) replaced Congress governments in the Hindi belt.

This was followed by the formation of the Janata Party government in 1977. It had brought together various non-Congress parties which had opposed the Emergency, and which went on to dethrone the Congress. Indira Gandhi lost even her own seat in that election. And he emerged as one of the shining stars of the Janata Party.

Again between 1987-89, he cast his lot with the anti-Congress forces, and worked with V.P. Singh, who came out of the Congress to take on Rajiv Gandhi (despite his brute majority of over 400 Lok Sabha seats, which had not even been clocked up by his grandfather and the country's first Prime Minister Jawaharlal Nehru), and went on to defeat him.

Fernandes also went on to make common cause with the Bharatiya Janata Party-led National Democratic Alliance in the period between 1998-2004 which was arraigned against the Congress.

Fernandes respected India's diversity and his fourth major contribution towards strengthening the country's democratic fibre was to reach out to those on the peripheries. Fernandes worked to bring Naxalites into the mainstream. He was in contact with Kashmiri militants to resolve the Kashmir tangle. He opened his doors to the Nagas and others from the North Eastern states, who felt alienated from the mainland, and to refugees from Tibet and Myanmar. The main gate at his Krishna Menon Marg home in Lutyens Delhi, when he was Union Defence Minister, was always open to these groups. And he ensured it was unmanned, despite the concerns of the security apparatus.

But if there was a development Fernandes could not live down—which could be called a turning point in his political career—it was in July 1979, when he defended Morarji Desai's

Janata Party government after it faced a no-confidence motion in Parliament. I still remember it was a Thursday. Fernandes gave an impassioned, brilliant performance, which only he could give. But by Sunday morning, he had done a turnaround at the instance of Madhu Limaye, a socialist colleague, and gone to the rebel camp, led by Chaudhary Charan Singh. Limaye had called the breakup of the Janata Party a historic necessity of the time. Prime Minister Desai subsequently submitted his resignation.

What could be more ironical than to have Fernandes, who was so opposed to the Congress, take a step which was to help bring down the first non-Congress government at the Centre? It paved the way for the return of Indira Gandhi in 1980. Even his family was baffled by why he did it.

It was then that he transited from being the fiery Fernandes to "George Sahab", and in the years that followed he became like "any other politician". He managed contradictions and navigated minefields, this time from within the system, and not outside it with the freedom to mount an attack, as he used to do in his earlier incarnation.

He would, however, sometimes display flashes of his earlier spirit. When he was Defence Minister under Atal Bihari Vajpayee (1998-2004), he went several times to the freezing heights of the Siachen glacier in Jammu and Kashmir to spend time with Indian soldiers.

Many of his colleagues were taken aback when he aligned with the BJP later, a party he had criticized for its ideology, after having formed the Samata Party in 1994.

Was it necessitated by the need for political survival and to retain his political relevance? The more charitable put this to a "no option" political scenario that existed at the time, given his visceral dislike of the Congress.

The Congress too loved to hate Fernandes, from the days of Indira Gandhi to Sonia Gandhi. There were those weeks in Parliament when the moment he would get up to speak as Defence Minister, his voice would be drowned by slogans of "coffin chor" being shouted by Congress members. This was a reference to the "coffin gate scam" in which allegations were made that the caskets bought by India in 2002 were of poor quality and exorbitantly priced. (The CBI, however, did not name Fernandes when it filed its chargesheet in the case in 2009.)

Fernandes was a skilled orator, in Parliament and outside it, a mass leader, but one who could also display a "personal touch" in reaching out to people individually. In 1977, my grandfather, a lawyer in Delhi, who did not know him, had written to him, saying that he suffered from ill health and despite repeated attempts he had not been able to get a telephone installed at his home. (I had suggested that he write to Fernandes soon after the Janata Party government came to power because he was known to be a "doer".) Within four days the telephone was installed, and Fernandes wrote him a personal three-line note.

George Fernandes was a hero to many, given his advocacy of the rights of the deprived, his fight to protect and restore democratic institutions, and his efforts to create an alternative to the dominant Indian National Congress. At the end of the day, it is heroes who keep the spirit of a nation alive, even though they are not perfect.

George Who Worked at Many Levels

Jaya Jaitly

George was so multifaceted that we will need about fifty chapters in a book to talk about each facet of him.

Often, when he was thinking of something he would be talking of something else and scribbling something else. I would ask him, "What are you doing?", and he would reply, with a smile, "My mind works at many levels." It was difficult to figure out how he was concentrating on so many things at once. This is what made him such a dynamic and vibrant personality. I can perhaps confidently claim that I was closest to him for over forty-two years; and I can say that everything worth knowing about humanity, about India, about politics, about our society, in its depth and seriousness and wisdom, I learnt from him. Also, I think I experienced the most misery, sadness and sorrow in the ups and downs that I had to face along with him. So, the legacy I have stored inside me at this stage, now that I am in my late seventies, is of understanding India in a wider sense than many. Being a woman and working with handicrafts and, therefore also being closely associated with our rural society (which people in big cities tend to forget and only theorise from one point of view), to what I learned from him, all affected me. The reason was it took me the whole morning to apply for a passport extension. I have been invited to Pakistan at the end of next month and Pakistan requires a one year validity visa, I had only nine or ten months left. However, because the earlier government wanted to attack George and pin him down and prove him as corrupt, (when he was probably the only incorruptible man in the country) he had to be proven as corrupt because they had to cancel out their Bofors scam with the false Tehelka scam. Finally, they could not get hold of him on tape so they got me and for the last thirteen years I have been embroiled in a case falsely put against me by the UPA government through the CBI. So, every time I want to go anywhere or want an extension of my passport, I have to go before the court and ask permission. I don't get a quick passport. I have to go through a whole rigmarole all over again and undertake that I will be away from only this date to this date.

For thirteen years I have spent nearly Rs 30 lakhs. My son has had to spend on lawyers and other things for a case which they have still not in thirteen years been able to prove that I accepted a bribe of Rs 2 lakhs. So, I do not know what economics or justice is involved in this, but the fact that I am fighting it cheerfully, is what George has taught me. The fact that I am there in court is thanks to George's legacy. But I look at it as a political fight, as he did about everything. He never took anything personally. Whether it was parliamentarians like, say, Mani Shankar Aiyar, or others who attacked him fiercely in Parliament, when they came out he would put his arm around them and say, "Come, let us have a cup of coffee", and they would apologize to him and later to me for no reason, saying that they were sorry but they "had to take the party line, though George is a great guy".

This is how he was. He never held any bitterness towards anyone. He would always have some sharp comment to make about his opponents. But if they came the next minute to ask him for help, he would do it with as much warmth and sincerity as he did for anybody else. Of course, as Anandji said, he was betrayed many times, but even that he would shrug off with a joke and say, "Well, you can never trust him. Let's see how far he goes." But again, it was part of life for him. He swallowed everything that came his way.

Why I got involved in politics, I was the most unlikely person, being a well-behaved wife of a well-behaved bureaucrat in Jammu and Kashmir. That's where we got to know Farooq Abdullah so closely, and I facilitated many meetings between George and Farooq, secret and otherwise. With Farooq and ourselves, it has been a forty-year friendship. There was nothing political about it. We finally came to Delhi and heard about this hero of the Emergency, and found my husband posted with him in the Ministry because George Sahab had said to the Governor of Kashmir at that time,

"I am going to be in the Industry Ministry. Give me an honest and capable officer, " the Governor, L.K. Jha, named my husband and that is how they got together. That friendship also lasted for as long as they were alive.

During that time in Kashmir, the Emergency was viewed differently because Sheikh Abdullah was against the Emergency. He was the only one who spoke against it, the first one, and so we had a different view. We were very free in opposing it even as bureaucrats, though we did not speak out. It was very clear in our household and with everyone we shared our views that this was not on and we were not going to accept it. So, we openly celebrated when Indira Gandhi lost and subsequently, we came to Delhi. Here we were landed in the office workspace of the great hero of the Emergency, George Fernandes.

As usual, I kept my distance because you don't meet your husband's boss for any social occasion of any importance, but he was kind enough to invite us for dinner which we politely accepted. But he was a serious human being who had no time for small talk. For the whole time at dinner nobody spoke and I thought, "My gosh, what a strange person he is, not uttering a word. Are we supposed to eat without speaking? " But afterwards, slowly he discovered that I was working in the handicrafts field and he used to sometimes come over to our house informally and talk about these things. Then I discovered that as the Industry Minister, he reserved over four hundred items for the small scale and cottage sector. He was already aware of the needs of this sector despite being preoccupied with trade unions and fighting the Emergency. Even at such high level activity, his mind and thoughts could easily focus beautifully on the rural aspect and the rural producer, rural livelihoods and how to protect them, the handloom weaver, the potter, the ironsmith, the blacksmith, anyone, he thought he must reserve sections for production for the small producer and cottage industry; next, what they could not manufacture, would be done by small-scale industry and what they could not do, would be done by large industry. So, he gave space to everybody as the Industry Minister, but he protected those who needed protection.

It was nearly eight years after this that we had a new textile policy and the whole thing was overturned, but during that time he was well aware that these were the sectors that needed protection. I was interested. I said, "This is the first time I have heard a politician talking about the sector that I have been working for in the rural areas, where there is sometimes no water or there is a drought." I was in Gujarat at that time which had undergone three years of drought. There was no fodder, the animals were dying and we went from home to home to identify which were the women who could do embroidery. Hundreds of women were then trained by us to work and earn a living, so that when the next drought came the women were the wage earners because they were still continuing their handicrafts, so if the cattle died and fodder was unavailable, families did not starve.

This was a very interesting revolution that took place when women became the saviours in the family, the earning members of the family, which created a greater respect for them. These kinds of activities, which are rural activities, helped a lot of social change in the village very silently. George Sahab recognized all this and my commitment. He wanted to channel that commitment into something larger. He had these unique ways of creating new ideas and ways of working which right up to the Konkan Railway, which I will touch upon briefly, came about. He said that what we need in the Hind Mazdoor Kisan Panchayat (HMKP) is to have a link created between the organized worker and the unorganized worker. That is because there is a limit to how much the organized worker can bargain for wage increases when his employer could turn him out and employ somebody from the village who is living hand to mouth and willing to work for any wage at all because he was not earning anything in the village.

Markets were changing, industrialization had come in, machine made goods were everywhere and there were no markets, or very few markets, left for the weavers and potters. So George said, "Let us build this link." He would go around with me to all the areas in Bombay where his trade unions were, where he would tell them they had to reach out to help their rural brothers and sisters. Therefore, taximen, rickshaw and auto rickshaw drivers, nurses in municipal hospitals, teachers in municipal schools, everyone who has to wear a uniform, should now want to access that cloth from weavers' homes. So that would link the weaver, give him a market, keep him in his home employed, and the organized worker would be reaching out, and in that help preserve his job. This was a wonderful unique thing. He would ask me to hold bazaars of this nature on the crafts theme and he would get his taximen to take the publicity pamphlets we had published, and ask them to keep it in their taxis. Every passenger that sat in the taxi would be handed over a leaflet by the taxidriver. This way we got free distribution of publicity when there was no money to put advertisements in newspapers.

These were the unique things George did after the Janata government fell and we got the Congress government again. During that time we worked extensively to link the organized worker with the unorganized worker. It worked for quite a while but then, as times changed, we found that even the unions were not quite used to all this. They had to be told that even the Coca Cola employees in the USA were demanding cotton uniforms and not polyester. By that time, of course, 1985, the 'polyester king' appeared on the scene and the new textile policy switched priority from employment as being the first goal of any policy to cheap cloth being the priority, employment coming second. We organized a huge programme with Chaudhary Charan Singh. I don't know if you know, it was his last programme before he died. In 1985 we were in Ahmedabad. Lakshmi Chand Jain who was earlier a member of the Handicrafts Board and Khadi Commission and Chaudhary Charan Singh arrived. George Sahab and I went from textile mill to textile mill in Ahmedabad, collecting all the polyester cloth and everybody was asked, like in Gandhi's time, to bring their polyester clothes and burn them. We had a big bonfire. There are still pictures in the media of Chaudhary Charan Singh with a long stick lighting that fire. It was quite a historic occasion.

These were the kind of things George Sahib did. If he was not a minister, he was active all the time. When he was a minister he was actively constructive. But he never let go of the many levels and many threads of work that he did. This drew me closer and closer to his work. During 1984 George Sahab, George Mathew and I, in the latter part of the terrible violence, set up the People's Relief Committee. I was not in the party and George Mathew was never in any party but we worked from the Janata Party office at

Jantar Mantar. We went to all those places where Sikhs had been attacked. We went to Bhogal. We walked through those burning buildings and everything else and then I went off to Farash Bazaar to a camp. For three months I worked in helping and rehabilitating the victims, sending for medicines, food and all kinds of things to Farash Bazaar which is across the Yamuna, driving off at seven in the morning, coming back at midnight. George Sahab in those days had made me like his lieutenant. He would write me notes: 'go and do this' and 'go and do that', 'where are you?', 'tell somebody such and such.' So, when his stenographers and PAs and other assistants and friends like Ravi were not around, the rest of the time I was supposed to be on constant duty doing all the political errands and other chores that he needed. He suddenly got frantic, saying, "Where are you? You are not available at all" and he got rather irritated and said, "Do you want to be Mother Teresa and clean up everybody else's dirt or do you want to remove those people who create that dirt?" That was the big question he asked me and which was his way of persuading me to join politics. He said, "Don't stand on the sidelines and sweep, clean and bandage everyone's wounds. Take up arms against those who create those sufferings, pain and hurt to our society." This was the way he persuaded me to enter the party and for thirty years I was in the party with him.

When he became the Railways Minister, again he brought out that concern for the handloom weavers by remembering that he had asked for the workers to wear uniforms. He called the entire Railway Board and put sets of cloth rolls, one pile made by the textile mills on one side and another pile made by handloom workers on the other side, which was also a mixture of polyester, because for uniforms you needed that sort of thing. He asked the Railway Board if any of them could make out which was handloom and which was mill cloth. They all came, put on their glasses, studied the display carefully and said that they couldn't tell the difference. He said that then they would order the bed sheets, pillow cases, blankets and the uniforms for the railwaymen out of handloom cloth. They had to agree because they found no difference in quality or anything. Unfortunately, corruption exists forever. Other officers found a way out. They would put the serial number of the power loom or the mill cloth on the order form but the description was of handloom. Nobody looks at the description. You look at the code or the serial number. At that time he was also the Special Minister for Kashmir. He was rushing off to Kashmir every other day in a situation where Farooq had resigned because he had been promised by V.P. Singh that Jagmohan wouldn't be sent as the Governor. In front of me Farooq phoned George and said, "I hear he is coming as the Governor. If he does, I'll quit." George phoned V.P. Singh, the Prime Minister, and said, "I hear Farooq saying this. Don't leave a gap between the central government and the people. Let their own representatives stay. Please don't send Jagmohan." V.P. Singh promised not to send Jagmohan and George, an hour later, took off for Manipur. By the time he landed in Imphal he heard the announcement that Jagmohan was posted as the Governor. So Farooq quit and George was left to deal with Jagmohan and the mess that followed.

While he was doing that, he was getting the Railway Board to do the handloom cloth, so everything went on, and apart from everything else he worked on the beautiful Konkan Railway idea. He got four state governments to work on the construction of the line from beginning to end. He got them to agree to have the Konkan Railway. The best way, he thought, was to do it in four stages. So there were four sections in which there was a four-pronged approach to build the railway in much less time, with an agreement with four different states and with four different parties. These were the kind of things he was able to do. The Konkan Railway was a wish fulfilled a hundred years later in which there were a large number of upstream and downstream jobs created. Today everyone who sits in that Konkan Railway train thanks George for it. Suresh Prabhu constantly talks about it and he may talk about it himself. He constantly sends me messages saying he has named this after George or that after George, that he is on the Konkan Railway and thinking about George. Suresh Prabhu is a very loving friend and he will reiterate it from a minister's position.

Thanks to Rajiv Gandhi, the then leader of opposition in Parliament, George was also made the Minister for Kashmir Affairs. George and Rajiv Gandhi were part of an all-party delegation to Srinagar during the height of early phase of militancy. Rajiv Gandhi was highly impressed when George with Ashok Subramanium got out of the fancy hotel where everyone was staying and shifted to a Railway guest house. He was also impressed by George's meetings and friendship with the militants and the Kashmiris. After the visit, Rajiv Gandhi recommended to V.P. Singh to give George the additional charge of Kashmir. This was very gracious of Rajiv Gandhi.

It is another sad story that a few years later, those very same people who were meeting him, who were moderates in their society, who were the bridge between the militants and the ordinary Kashmiris, were all shot dead because they were meeting George. People like Dr Abdul Ahad Guru, a leading physician, were shot dead. It is all recorded in history.

At that time, the relationship between the Congress and the V.P. Singh government was really not bad. Rajesh Pilot took over later when V.P. Singh's government went and he used to come over and the three of us would talk about how to carry on George's commendable work in Kashmir.

After this came the Defence Ministry which was another long story. George's life is so full of stories that even when he taught something it was in the form of a story. He would relate a story that would go on for an hour and a half or two hours. Once all night he told me about how they arranged the Baroda Dynamite plan. All night he sat up in a hotel in Baroda with his union colleagues, reiterating and telling us this whole tale. When he told it to you like a story, you never forgot a word of it. Suddenly in the middle of it all he started talking about national security because we were concerned with Tibet, we were concerned with Burma, where there was no democracy. We had these huge international conferences which Anand was very much a part of, where we revived people's awareness and interest in the crucial need for India to keep Tibet as a buffer zone of peace, which for the Socialists had been a badge of honour to carry on for the Tibetans for so long. We never for a minute gave up and when George thought that things were lagging as he did when he came back once from a meeting which Petra Kelly and Gert Bastion had organized in Germany he said, "We are organizing an international conference in August." Suddenly it was upon me to organize such a big conference. I had never organized a conference in my life. It became such a big story because the government foolishly asked Gyani Zail Singh not to come and in the morning the newspapers said: "Gyani Zail Singh told not to come". I said, "Here, our conference is made." Sure enough, Gyaniji came and it was a big story and we take pride that maybe five per cent of the effect of that conference was His Holiness getting the Nobel Prize that year.

These are all stories, interconnected. You cannot disassociate and talk of only one thing with George because he was doing multiple layers of work and multiple levels of work. He was doing ten things at the same time and wanting to do twenty more things. People said that he should retire and write his memoirs but he said, "You will have to take me out feet first." He could never sit still. There was no retirement for somebody who never claimed that he ever had a job. In this case when he was asked to take over the Defence Ministry, he was very hesitant. People think that he wanted to go to Parliament to become a minister. I have read some nasty articles saying he couldn't keep away from power, but each time he had refused to go into the Ministry. There are historical records of this. He didn't join the Janata Party government immediately. In the Railways, he took three or four days to join because he told V.P. Singh, "How can I sit across the table from people whom I fought against in the Railway Strike?" For the Defence Ministry he said, "Defence! How will I face all these Army officers in their crisp starched suits? Look at me in my *kurta pyjama*." He did not want to. People like Jaswant Singh, Advaniji, all came and literally cried that they could not form a government without him. Vajpayee sent a message saying, "I will go to the President and say that I am not forming a government unless you are there." This was how he was pushed in every time and I am witness to this. So it really hurts when George never sought power and position for himself yet everybody here says and writes such things. It can be very sad for those of us who know him better.

I phoned him one morning at about six thirty and I said, "You know, I have been thinking that you do not want to join the Defence Ministry because of the uniforms and stiffness, but have you thought that we as a party have talked about national security? Here is your opportunity to turn things around." The

Foreign Ministry was always guiding policy about China, about Tibet, about Burma, because they were constantly succumbing to China because of the old Nehruvian fondness for them and fears of 1962. I said that here was a chance for him to perhaps change their mindset. He accepted that argument and finally agreed to be the Defence Minister. He walked in and immediately changed all kinds of rules because he found Parliament questions coming about corruption. He immediately passed an order that there will be boxes for complaints of corruption which had to be signed properly by a person, nothing anonymous, and that he would keep the keys in his own pocket for these boxes and he would read these himself. Jayant Malhotra from Parliament wrote about re-opening of Bofors that had been banned but they changed the name and there were some supplies needed. The guns were all here. They were unfortunately rotting. They were perfectly good guns but because dealing with that company was banned, they were all useless and the Army wanted those guns to be used. So he reopened the whole idea and when he called for the file, the interesting thing that happened was that Vajpayee phoned him and said, "Leave that file alone."

Somehow word got around that he was going into the Bofors scam and not the Bofors spare parts. In any case, he ordered those spare parts and also decided that if anybody was talking about corruption then from Rajiv Gandhi's time to his own time and onwards, the CAG and Vigilance would both study any orders, any deals over Rs. 75 crore. Both these things actually set off alarm bells and that's what scared many people. I may point out and say, "Oh well, the Congress did this and somebody did that." But actually, I believe that even deeper than the Congress there is a very hard layer of arms dealers whose names we never hear and whose work we do not know, who work in all kinds of ways, to the extent that some Congress parliamentarian came to me and said, "Did you know that you were the most popular lady in Delhi? People would pay Rs. 25 lakhs just to have a cup of tea with you." This meant that they could show from the outside that they were free with me and get a hefty sum from some arms supplier for that and they could go out and pretend that they talked to me about expediting a file, which would never see at all.

Both George Sahab and I were completely innocent about this kind of situation because other than the fight against Bofors he had not involved himself with the Defence Ministry at all. The fight about the HDW Submarine was there but it was only on the wrongdoing, not about the supplies or the equipment or the quality of equipment or who ordered or how much it cost. These were not his concern. When this happened and they found that they could not get through this barrier which George had put up to prevent corruption in the Defence Ministry, that's when they got after both him and me. He had to go through CBI enquiries and cases and, as I said in the beginning, I am still at it.

Therefore, it is very difficult to say what exactly George Fernandes's legacy is. One brief footnote is that during the Defence Ministry time, when I was accused of guiding him in various deals, I had actually asked him if they could buy something from the handicrafts sector. He said, "Yes, have an exhibition inside the Ministry." I got government agencies to set up an exhibition where we found that the Army was actually buying shoes for Rs 1200 when you could get them from Agra from shoemakers for Rs 400; that you could have handmade paper files instead of industry made files. The Army actually placed several orders which never came about because they finally attacked George Sahab and the Army that the whole Defence Ministry froze even in ordering shoes and files. And then I was accused of bribery in defence deals. These are the kind of legacies that you learnt to fight, that you learn to accept, you learnt to be actually proud of because I see this as a fight against corruption. It is a fearless fight. I don't care what the court says or does and I don't care when people say that it must be harassment. I do not feel harassed. Yes, it is irritating as a few hours in a day get wasted.

However, it is a battle and one which I am proud to fight because it is, as I said, part of the legacy which George has left in all of us. I don't feel despondent the way Farooq felt and shed tears about it because I feel if all of us have in us the fight, the creativity and the optimism that George always had, then we should never bow down or feel sad. This is as much our country as everybody else's. We have a right just as the next man or woman to fight or hold our heads up and uphold what we believe in, and I strongly believe in humanity itself, let alone the people of India. We are secular, we are peace loving, including in Kashmir. Just yesterday, a crafts person told me, "Ninety-two per cent of the Kashmiris want to be at peace and want to remain within India. What can we do? We can't speak out because if we speak out we are hit by the militants, and if we don't, we are hit by the government. Tell us what to do. All we want in Kashmir is to be able to carry on our lives peacefully." This is something we need to hear and I wish people like Farooq lent an ear to that and spoke out about that. It is not about parties. It is about our country and Kashmir as a part of our country. "They are ordinary people", my Kashmiri friend says; "There are two or three small townships which are militant, at most two or three hundred people in Kashmir are militant. The rest are all of us, " they say, "you should see all these Hurriyats and other people. They have little, petty leaders under the Hurriyat who have four-storey houses with nine air conditioners, twenty-five private and government guards and all their relatives in government jobs in Kashmir."

Who is going to speak out about these realities? They say we all know and if somebody gives a call for a *bandh*, they all say, "*Haan, haan, woh chaar chaar AC wala bol raha hai, dus AC wala bol raha hai.*" They mock them but they are still imprisoned by them in the sense that they don't know when, if they speak out, they are going to be shot, and somebody will blame the Army, somebody will blame somebody else, and so it goes on. I hear this every single day from simple crafts people with whom I have worked for thirty years, from Kashmir, who through curfew, storm or *bandh*, will come to me and speak like this. We need to reach out to those ordinary people. I think there is nothing to be despondent about. That is what George always taught me and I hope I can share that.

Leader of the Masses

K.C. Tyagi

I first heard George Sahab during my student days in 1969, in my home town Ghaziabad. He addressed a political party meeting and I was there. In 1967 George Sahab had defeated S.K. Patil, the Congress Party stalwart, in Mumbai and attained a nationwide reputation. There was too much excitement on the dais and among the people when he came to Ghaziabad. It was the peak of the anti-Congressism in the aftermath of Dr Lohia's death. After George Sahab's speech, we felt assured that the legacy of that moment would never come to an end. Although it was an urban constituency the candidate from our party won the election. Since I had never been a part of the trade union movement, my understanding about political activists was that their discussions centred around only those questions related to wage increase or gratuity and such issues. However, George Sahab expressed his opinion concerning all issues, national and international. He made a prophetic statement that there would be a split in the Congress Party and thereafter, there would be a big consolidation among the socialists.

Many events took place over the course of time that followed and he lost the elections in 1971. George Sahab was not made for elections. People who contest elections also have a caste and a locality where they concentrate. However, George was made for the entire humanity. He was made for wherever there is trouble, injustice, oppression and inequality in the world.

We joined the Lok Dal in 1974 and our office was in Vithalbhai Patel House. Some of our old time friends were here. The office of the Lok Dal was in numbers one and two and the office of the Socialist Party was in thirteen and fourteen or fourteen and fifteen. George

Sahab was the President and Surendra Mohanji was the General Secretary. In this way and also in connection with the anti-Congress movement, we used to get an opportunity to observe him closely and listen to him. The Emergency was the manifestation of the movement of the Railway workers that took place in independent India and the way the ruling party revealed their intentions and their inclination to crush it. That was the beginning of both Indira Gandhi's temperament and how she contemplated crushing any probable significant people's movement, which she demonstrated in imprisonments during the Rail Strike. I may say that if the Rail Strike had not taken place under the leadership of George Fernandes, there would probably not have been an Emergency in the country. This was its beginning and the intentions to counter that Rail Strike were like the kind of intentions a Commander-in-Chief of India can have during a war with Pakistan.

It was beginning to seem as if under the leadership of Mrs Gandhi, the ruling party was determined to crush the people's movements. These organized efforts for opposition unity were also made in those days. However, George Sahab always kept his distance. As a socialist of repute, he wanted to keep the questions of the Socialist Movement, its identity, its characteristic features and framework distinct. Even when the Janata Party was formed he was against it. He said that there was no need of the Janata Party and even wrote a letter from the prison, which his close friends knew about. He was even against contesting in the elections. He wrote that the elections of 1977 did not mean a thing in the ongoing Emergency, there would be a high level of rigging and Mrs Gandhi's ambitions of imposing capital punishment would be accomplished. I was glad that George Sahab was proved wrong in this matter.

For some time during the Emergency we got an opportunity to lend a hand in his groundwork programmes. Influenced by him, the three of us, his old friend and our senior comrade, Satyadev Tripathi, me and a friend of mine, Rajendra Choudhary, who is presently with the Samajwadi Party, made up our minds to use a bomb. Our fourth ally was S. Bhadoriya who, following his father's footsteps, had worked briefly on it in Itawah. However, we had become anxious due to Choudhary Charan Singh's character, conduct and way of working. We could not touch a bomb for fear of being expelled from the party by Choudhary Sahab who was a hardcore Gandhian, and therefore, could not be a part of George Fernandes's scheme which involved a bomb, although we were young and wanted to do something like that. Also, there were many ideological disputes among the socialists regarding that period. George Fernandes had digressed from the conventional stream of the socialist movement, which is Gandhian as he believed that the ruling party was so cruel, ruthless and despotic that it should be got rid of by any means. This also included dynamite, which was later part of it.

We used to visit the courts with Satyadev Tripathi and a few friends when the Emergency was lifted. That was from where he won the elections. Many of our associates here took part in that election. While living in Vithalbhai Patel House, we came to know that George was coming to visit. In the meantime, Morarji Desai had become the Prime Minister and he had issued a statement, "Let us forgive and forget." Upon his release from prison, George, probably soon after oath-taking, had come to VP House and the subject of his entire speech was, "How can I forgive and how can I forget?" He delivered an hour long speech on that subject and the misdeeds of Indira Gandhi during the Emergency, the humiliation faced by his mother and his brother, how Jayaparakash Narayan's health suffered during that time and the injustice done towards the families of thousands of activists, were the contents of his historical speech, "How can we forgive and how can we forget?"

Later, after 1980, being in the same party, I got an opportunity to be associated with his programmes and to observe him at a close range. I do not want to say anything controversial. However, thereafter there was no leader born in independent India who had the desire for social and economic transformation and who had the courage to fulfil it. Also, not on only one front but on a thousand fronts. In the meantime, a few days ago I got the opportunity to visit certain parts of Jammu and Kashmir and also in the context of the Citizenship Amendment Bill in the North East. Actually if sometimes we conduct ourselves and behave against the Act we are at a risk of losing our integrity and it also leads to political loss. I had never imagined that Jayaprakash would ever support plebiscite. It was big news for me.

I got the opportunity to read a book sometime back in which the Kashmiris blame all three, Jinnah, Jawaharlal and Sheikh Abdullah for their ruin. They have expressed gratitude towards only one person who fought for their independence till his last day, Jayaprakash. This was big news. His writing of those days reveals that he was alone besides Dr Lohia who was there in any case. He sent many of his representatives during that time, and that was when I went to the North East. In 1952 Rishang Kieshing was the first MP of the Socialist Party from Manipur. Many of my learned friends with a better memory than mine will support my claim. When I went the other day I met my associates there who later joined the Congress, which is a separate story and is not my subject. There are dozens of places there also where the kind of personality that Jayaprakash had could be known through Patna, Kadamkuan, GPF, where our associates got to hear him. Another side to Jayaprakash was that he interacted with Lal Denga and the people of the North East.

It would not be an exaggeration to say that after Gandhi and Patel if there was any man who worked for national integration, it was George Fernandes. Which mainstream political leader goes to Kashmir? There is a *sher* from Dushyant Kumar's *ghazal*:

Lahu lahaan nazaaron ka zikr aaya toh
Shareef log uthe door ja ke baith gaye.

So when Kashmir or the North East gets mentioned, the gentry of Delhi hesitates, fears and avoids even debating on it. George was there, Farooq Sahab was to come later, and he was the lone man in V.P. Singh's government and also in Morarjibhai's government, whose commitment towards the cause of Kashmir stood even after he allied with the BJP. However it was never fulfilled. It changed to autonomy. George continuously made efforts for it. Similarly for the North East where George Sahab worked with total dedication and diligence, whereas, both the socialists and anti-socialists of these times do not even wish to visit the North East as there are fewer tourist attractions there.

Once I had the opportunity to travel with him when the tobacco producers of Guntur wrote to Choudhary Charan Singh about their problems asking him to come, and he deputed George Sahab to go on his behalf. Other associates have had more such experiences. Going by train on a free ticket, we stopped over en route at Ratlam where he addressed a small group of eighteen persons for two hours speaking non-stop. The leaders of today need a high profile gathering, publicity, expenditure and in addition, an arrangement of a coterie of two dozen leaders around them who croon about how they are greater than God, next to Allah and so on. George Sahab spoke without any introduction. It was dark and a lamp was lit as for some reason there was no electricity at Ratlam. Our journey began there and we then went to Guntur. It was then that I came to know about his practice of finishing dinner by eight-thirty if he could, and if not, he would not eat anything later, only drank milk. Anyway, he addressed the farmers of Guntur. He used to try to get many jobs done at the same time. He then went to Vijayawada and addressed the long time supporters of Dr Lohia who were running an initiative to promote Hindi. Thereafter, he went to Hyderabad where there used to be an office of the Socialist Party. He socialized with dozens of people there who were close to him and we returned after four days. I found this trip unnecessary as it would not have led to any immediate result. However, sitting and gossiping in office, assaulting the character of leaders or commenting on them was not George Fernandes's nature. His colleagues may know about it. He kept aloof from the common practice among youth who chat for hours on end. Even if he heard anybody being criticized, he just listened to it but would not give his approval or encourage it.

Many associates may have various rich memories, nonetheless. When Bhai Anandji and Vijayji went to Nepal they came to know that causing major embarrassment to the Government of Nepal, he had made a plan to go to China from there. His rebellious attitude was to the extent of anarchism and it attracted young people like us. We felt that George Fernandes should be emulated and there was no need to be organized. If one is protesting against institutionalized systems then a systematic revolt has no meaning. Anarchy has to be a part of it. Therefore, George Fernandes, in spite of associating himself with the likes of S.M. Joshi and the calm and composed Surendra Mohanji, stood apart from them. Many of us have been with Madhu Limaye, and there was not a single event in the course of his day which bore any similarity with George's. Nevertheless, they were together till he breathed his last, in spite of unpleasant decisions.

George and Surendra Mohanji used to occupy separate rooms in numbers fourteen-fifteen. I do not wish to create a controversy by comparing their personalities, however, they never interacted with each other. There was no conversation between them. The result of this further developed in the socialist movement of today. The fact was that they had different ways of working, but I would like to say from the depth of my heart that while living amidst democratic organizations having no caste affiliations, there has been no person born like George Fernandes. To engage in politics now one needs to have a caste, which he did not have. He was a Roman Catholic and these days there is a proliferation of newer and newer forms of religions, which George Fernandes also went through. I recall post-Godhra, his loved ones did not approve of his new avatar, which they should not have in any case, as George Fernandes was not Allah after all and there could be a disagreement with him and his opinions. However, he successfully completed the work that he was meant to do.

The way North Indians are humiliated today, he ran the trade union also not just for wage increase. Anyone who wants to be a taxi driver or buy a taxi is unable to get a loan in Mumbai. A bank was created by him and it was ensured that any driver, whether North Indian or South Indian, could enrol as a member of the union and would get a vehicle loan at the lowest rate of interest with guarantee. There had always been an absence of a constructive role amongst socialists. On stage they can reduce everything from Section 144 to Jawaharlal Nehru to ashes, but if there was any constructive work done by a socialist, it was only George Fernandes. Even today, the office at Charni Road stands. A few days ago, I met his successor Sarad Rao and his son. I wish to inform you that even though George Fernandes may not have left a legacy and did not have a dynasty on the lines of Jawaharlal and other leaders, his splendour was such that in the strike last week during which Mumbai came to a standstill for a week, Sarad Rao's son Sasank Rao, got BEST, Municipal Corporation and the Taximen Union to stage the biggest strike ever. So George Fernandes may not be any more, a lot of work will continue to be done in his memory in various places.

Making profound observations in the middle of casual conversations, he once told us that initiatives should be taken with respect to artisans' trade. While acting as the Railway Minister, he propagated Gandhian economics concerning artisan trade by introducing *kulhars* in the railways, which was an innovation in itself. We had organized a big programme at Ferozshah Kotla in Delhi. I got glimpses of him during the Emergency. When he was arrested, from Willy Brandt to half a dozen heads of state, all categorically warned Indira Gandhi against any harm done to him. It was believed that George would be killed upon arrest. Thousands of people used to be in constant touch with the BBC and the German Embassy, and I was one of them. Even before the Police entered to arrest George, the BBC reported that he had been arrested.

Four or five years back, a minister from the UPA government went on a tour to Sweden, Norway, etc. Upon his return he reported that two Prime Ministers had asked, "How is George?" Two Prime Ministers had asked a minister about George. The international form of socialism was the network of Prime Ministers, but in spite of personal differences, George Sahab was internationally recognized as the most vigorous and glorious socialist leader.

The way George created a space for himself in the form of a miracle, in the form of people's struggles and in the form of a complete human being, a radical humanist, will be remembered in history. One does not expect much from such strong men, everyone leads his life in his own way. Lohiaji did not have a child and neither did Jayaprakash, but millions of people remember them on one pretext or another. Some people have great children who even displace them at times. Therefore, whenever secularism is discussed the wrong people talk about it who may have gone with the BJP. However, after the Godhra incident occurred, it was George Fernandes who led the military march holding the flag on the roads of Baroda and Ahmedabad. I do not say this to defend the politics of NDA. I merely wish to mention George Fernandes's personality. Whenever human rights are discussed, our friends from Tibet are here and Tibet has mourned more than India; they felt as if a prominent leader of Tibet had passed away. The simple life he led will influence many generations to come.

Without elaborating further on what I am saying about the brief time I spent with him, I would like to pay a tribute to him and would also like to request everyone to preserve some of his memories every year because a George Fernandes is not born every day. In future, there will be no one like him because to be like George Fernandes one has to get used to dying. George used to die every day and be ready to face death. Therefore, a chain of his memories will be maintained by Matthew Sahab for which people like us shall be prepared to play any role.

Real Hero of Emergency

Suresh Prabhu

We need to remember someone when we are likely to forget him, but a person like George Sahab can never be forgotten for the kind of work he did, multifarious activities with full dedication, commitment, leadership and the kind of emotive support he could get from all sections of society, not just in India but all over the world, is simply phenomenal.

Therefore, he will always be remembered and that we owe to his great work and that is how we carry his legacy forward. As you want me to tell you something about George Sahab, I could never even imagine I would ever even meet him in person. As a student when he fought his first election in 1967 in Mumbai, he defeated S.K. Patil. At that time I was too young but I was still enamoured by his personality. Then, when I was in college, he started his great phenomenon called Mumbai *Bandh*. One strike that he organized for the municipal workers continued for a long time and I attended one of the public meetings that he used to have, I think, every alternate day or every few days, because the strike was going on for a longer period. He spoke for about two or three hours non-stop. He was speaking less about the Municipal workers who were all there wanting to know when the strike would be called off or would be successfully concluded. He was giving them different kinds of ideas. What is more important is that despite the fact that the workers were present because of the strike, not a single person ever got bored or wanted to leave. They were fully engaged in what George Sahab was saying and he was moving from one subject to another, sometimes going into global issues, coming back to Mumbai politics, everything, and he was just playing it so well. That was one of his first few lectures I heard.

Later on, as he said, in the Emergency, I was also a small participant in the Emergency movement, but he was a real hero. I think no one had really opposed the Emergency the way he did. He organized so many things and when he was arrested, that of course is very well known how he was arrested in the church and everything. But later, while he was in jail he won that famous election. *Jail ka taala tootega, George Fernandes jeetega*, and he actually won, became Industries Minister and then ensured that Coca Cola went away from India. I think they started a drink called Seventy Seven that time to remember the spirit of 1977.

Actually, I don't know anyone who has been a mobilizer of masses of that kind, organizer of a movement of a type that he did during the Emergency, and suddenly changing roles to be a Minister and doing such a great job in the Ministry. He was the Railways Minister. I also became the Railways Minister many years after him. Konkan Railways, where I was elected in the Parliament four times would not have been possible but for George Sahab. He steamrolled, that was his quality. If anybody came in the way he would make sure to remove them and actually created an organization, the first of its kind which talked about creating special purpose vehicles, creating infrastructure and raising issues. He actually created that office, handpicked Sreedharan and made it possible. It is a different story that those who had opposed that concept used that as a political plan to win elections after that. It is the factual position. In fact, George Sahab came once to my constituency amid opposition from his comrades and colleagues and he said, "No, I will come and tell the truth." He came there to campaign for my election.

I created an institution in Goa called Tunnels. Konkan Railways created it for creating a global institute, connected to and tied up with the Italian Government. I said that it is the right institute to immortalize this great contribution, because you need a tunnel when there is a block, you cannot remove it but you use a tunnel to get through. That was George Sahab because he could get rid of everything that came in his way and made sure he reached his destination. He was a person who could speak many languages. I remember those days when Ramakrishna Hegde was his close friend. He used to live in Lodhi Estate. He often visited

Ramakrishna Hegde's house and it was one of the greatest feats to listen to George Sahab's various ideas on every subject on which he had his own opinion and ideas, and such great ideas.

In fact, he became the Convenor of the NDA and I think, people say that he was very individualistic and could not work as a team, but George Sahab was the greatest asset of the NDA. Atalji acknowledged it many times and he ran it so well that the NDA never had a problem. It is a different matter that some came in and some went out, but he was the guiding force under Atalji's leadership. That government spread completely false propaganda against him which had nothing to do with reality, completely motivated, and despite that George Sahab remained the greatest leader and he will continue to be that.

I remember, he was the Defence Minister. If you went to his house, the Defence Minister who is supposed to defend everybody else, he never had a single police personnel to defend him at the main gate. Jayaji used to be there and I went there sometimes for dinner with my wife, a dog would be sitting there and George Sahab would have some friends from Tibet. They used to be staying there because in any case they were refugees from their homeland but they had a real home in George Sahab's house. That was George Sahab. He never bothered about anybody. He had gone frequently to different locations as Raksha Mantri, and he changed that Raksha Mantri incidentally. The name Raksha Mantri has been changed because of George Sahab. Otherwise we called it Defence Minister till recently, till he became the Raksha Mantri, and that is something only he could do. He never worried, never bothered, believed in what he believed in and to listen to his speeches in the Parliament was a real treat. He invariably spoke in Hindi and that is something I am trying to learn from him. He was fluent in English and many other languages but made it a point to speak in Hindi, and what speeches they were you would say if you heard the speeches of George Sahab in Shivaji Park that I heard. When he spoke in Parliament he spoke differently as a Minister and as the Opposition. That is something one must learn, how to switch roles from one to another and at the same time do justice to each role as required.

I think unfortunately George Sahab and Atalji, both suffered a lot in the end but as one said that they were suffering in different ways. Atalji knew everything but physically he was sick. George Sahab was probably fine bodily but had a problem remembering many things. That was the sad part of a great leader. I saw both Atalji and George Sahab, both in their own right, great leaders and the close proximity that George Sahab had with so many people and so many leaders was incredible. In fact, I was one of the junior-most and he used to treat me as if I was his oldest friend for years, although I had not known him for that long. His affection, respect, giving space to people, allowing them and also at the same time supporting them was incredible.

In Mumbai of course, he created even the New India Cooperative Bank. I was also the Chairman of the Saraswat Bank so I had also known that he could understand the importance of creating so many institutions and one of the greatest things was that he never got attached to them. All the trade unions in Mumbai, the important ones were virtually created by him. Somebody else ran them but he never bothered and told them to do what they could as it was not his business, it was his mission. Therefore, many activities he did, and I remember Willy Brandt and how close we were as friends. The way he was arrested when Willy Brandt took up that issue and said that he should not be harmed.

So you can imagine one of the greatest leaders and we can sometimes wonder whether one really knew him. If you are really saying 'the George I knew' is what you wanted people to speak about, every time you speak about what you knew of him suddenly you realize how much you don't know of him. A person like him had so much in that one body, one human mind that it is difficult to really comprehend him, because he could really present himself the way the other person wanted him to do it. He would be available to you as a friend, he would be available to you as a leader, as a colleague, as a student or a teacher. So he could present himself as the circumstances demanded. As I said, from a trade unionist to anti-Emergency activist to a Member of Parliament, opposition leader to minister. He could play so many roles at different times as the time demanded and time needed.

I would call him one of the greatest leaders who has ever lived in India and one of the great sons of India. I think we should all try to do as much as possible. Jayaji, of course, has done a great thing single-handedly. For no fault of hers sometimes she has even handled difficult unnecessary issues, but she has been one of the greatest carriers of his legacy along with him. I cannot even claim to be closer to what George Sahab was. Of course, whatever we can do in our own small way, should be done. But anyway if you ask such a person like George Sahab what we should do in his memory, he would say, "Don't do anything." He would not want anything, he did not want anything in his own life and I am sure that he did not want anything after he died. I was just mentioning that when he was the Raksha Mantri he would go to different locations. He went to Kargil I don't know how many times. He would come back to office, sleep in South Block in his office, get ready and again go out. When I say ready, it was nothing, he would use the same clothes for probably many days. A person from Mumbai from Goregaon, Madhu Wadekar gave me a story. When George Sahab used to go to the workers, he needed to change and Madhu pointed out that he needed to change his kurta. As he did not have any other, they stitched something for him which he carried. However, at the next destination, when he checked, he said he didn't know where it was and had probably lost it. So he was someone who was like this, who never bothered about worldly possessions, never bothered about his own personality, never bothered about his legacy. Such selfless dedication for the cause of the nation.

All of us know about the great Chikmagalur election. The way he went there and from nothing, nowhere he could garner so many people. Of course, he could speak many languages, as I said. Tulu was probably his mother tongue. It is difficult to say what his mother tongue was because he used so many and spoke all languages fluently. But in Chikmagalur it was Kannadiga and he could speak any language and it almost made Indira Gandhi lose that election. So we will never be able to forget him.

One Can Never Forget George Fernandes

Sumit Chakravartty

It is very difficult for me to speak about George Sahab because for the last few years that he was indisposed and virtually bedridden, I did not have a chance to meet him. That was because I did not want to see a person so active and dynamic, being reduced to the condition in which he was. However, my association with George Sahab started when I first met him way back in 1968 when he had come to Delhi after emerging as a giant slayer, defeating S.K. Patil a year earlier, and becoming a member of the Lok Sabha. There was a meeting organized by the Samajwadi Yuvajan Sabha on the terrace of the flat in North Avenue where he was staying, and the discussion was on what steps should be taken to rejuvenate the Socialist Movement, especially after the emergence of the Shiv Sena in the city of Bombay, now called Mumbai. George Sahab had said at that meeting that the slogan which was raised by the Shiv Sena was: '*Laal jhandaa jalaa do, George Fernandes ko bhagaa do*.' The point is: this was a phenomenon which was rising at that particular point of time and it was necessary to fight this menace. We all spoke there briefly but that was the ambience in which the meeting took place.

Subsequently, I had the opportunity to meet George Sahab several times. Of course, during the Emergency what he did was something phenomenal and I don't have to go into those details, except to say that whatever he did at that particular point of time for the cause of human rights and democracy, I do not know, Dr George Matthew will be able to correct me, whether not everything, but at least a substantial portion of that has been written. I think, if it is not, we should try to do that. C.G.K. Reddy has written about it, but not George Sahab. He was very reticent, I found on many occasions, to speak about that period, presumably because of various reasons.

I had a close association with him during the time of the Janata Dal Government led by V.P. Singh in 1989-90. We had occasions to discuss at length how the situation would shape in the coming days. Here I would like to mention one thing which has been referred to, but not gone into in detail. Among all his contributions in public life, one of the most important contributions was—unfortunately which he could not continue with because of other reasons—what he did in Kashmir in January, 1990. By the end of 1989 there was an insurgency in Kashmir which continues to this day. George Sahab had then gone to Kashmir, got in touch with some of the militants, young people, and he was in the process of starting a dialogue with them. Unfortunately, he had to be called back for reasons best known to the people who were then in power. This was perhaps because they had changed tack and decided to send at that point of time a person who had definitely proved his administrative capabilities, Jagmohan, but who wanted to follow a different course obviously with the Centre's concurrence. Farooq Abdullah will be able to dilate on that in depth. However, he (Jagmohan) was not suited for what was the demand of that time: to start a channel of dialogue with the young people who had been alienated from the mainstream and were part of the insurgency, which later on took a much bigger shape. In fact, on the occasion of George Sahab's sixtieth birth anniversary function in New Delhi where V.P. Singh and others were present, this point was raised. V.P. Singh subsequently said, "This is a flaw which I concede." It is now of no use to speculate on what would have happened had George Sahab been allowed to continue with that assignment; probably things would have then changed for the better in Kashmir. That is my opinion.

So, George Fernandes's contribution and potential was definitely much more than we can imagine. The Tibetan presence here is so overwhelming and everyone knows how much he did to help the Tibetan cause. But I am also reminded of George Sahab's total support for the movement for democracy in Burma. In fact, we had set up a Friends of Burma organization which functioned from George Sahab's residence, apart from the fact that the young students of Burma also had their own office in George Sahab's place, even when he was a Minister in the Union Cabinet. That was his open-door policy. He did not have a gate in his residence at that time. Subsequently, because of security reasons, a gate was constructed. But in reality there was no gate at his residence on Krishna Menon Marg, it was really an open house. We could go in and come out anytime.

I distinctly remember, after the 1998 elections when the BJP, not alone but as a leader of the NDA, was about to form the government, I had to go to George Sahab's place to deliver a letter. After I had done so, he asked me to sit down and queried, "What should I do?" That is, his query was whether he should join the Union Government or not. My reply was clear. I said, "It is for you to decide. I have no problem with the BJP, but my problem is with the RSS and I don't have to dilate on that, you know that much better." His answer was very significant. He said, "I fully agree with you, Sumit." Subsequently what happened is a different matter, but what I am trying to impress upon you, which all of you know, was his inherent, innate democratic credentials. He was a democrat to the core. He would listen to everyone and then decide on his own course of action. This one has seen during the Emergency, and also subsequently on many other occasions.

So many memories come flooding in. Unfortunately, time is short. One cannot write or say much, except to point out one thing about his democratic credentials. There was, after the new economic policies were initiated in 1991, a meeting at Vithalbhai Patel House, where a Leftist economist who was also an activist, scathingly attacked Mrs Gandhi, going to the extent of saying that she had ensured that in her constituency of Rae Barely and the neighbouring constituency of Amethi, maximum foreign exchange was brought in through the Jazeera pipeline. I was somewhat puzzled and wondered how that could be. After coming back to office, I rang George Sahab and told him that this was what had been mentioned by the gentleman there. He immediately said: "No, this is not an issue which one can raise. This is a pipeline which is necessary for the country. If it goes through those constituencies, we cannot object to that." Now, this shows that he was used to going into the depth of every issue and then taking the best decision in the national interest.

As the Defence Minister, while meeting him at his residence or at the South Block, one had found him to be extremely meticulous. In fact, in May 1998 when the Pokhran II tests were carried out, he had called me at his residence in the morning. I had then an appointment with him. We were discussing the functioning of the Defence Ministry, the kind of activities he was engaged in and all that. Just by chance, it was not my intention, the nuclear question came up and his reply was: "That is a different issue. Let us not go into the nuclear question. Let us discuss other things." It was only that much he told me then. He was able to keep all the secrets to himself, unlike many of today's leaders. You know whatever is going on, what has happened in the Cabinet. In fact, the person who had all along, even during and soon after the Emergency spoken out against this, was our former President, Pranab Mukherjee. I once told him, "Now everyone is saying what happened in the Cabinet. This person went out because of nature's call and all that." To that Pranab Babu said, "Look, as far as I am concerned, whatever happens in the Cabinet can be discussed only after I die. It will go with me to the grave or the cremation ground. I cannot and will never divulge it." The same applied to George Sahab.

He had so many sterling qualities and that is why I think we should remember a person who has done so much for the country in a broad sense. He was the only Defence Minister who undertook so many trips to the Siachen Glacier to meet the troops. You should hear from the troops the great regard they had for George Sahab. It is not only activists but everyone who came into contact with him was influenced by him, myself included. One can never forget him.

George—The Civil Libertarian

Ravi Nair

I will focus on the George Fernandes that I knew, in terms of the civil liberties and human rights issues that he undertook. I was initially associated with him politically; my political association started with him because of civil liberties concerns. I first went and met him along with a very senior Gandhian the late Mr Ramadhar, in the early 1970s. He was not the typical Gandhian. He believed that we had to adopt the Chinese method of development; in terms of collective and cooperative farms and other things that many of us would not find palatable to speak about today. But he was somebody who put himself out for public causes unlike many other 'official Gandhians' who run their Gandhian institutions like medieval monasteries or *mutts* and did nothing to foster Gandhiji's civil disobedience teachings against unjust government policies.

In the early 1970s, many young people in Bengal, Bihar, Punjab and Andhra Pradesh were arrested under the guise of combating Naxalism. Several innocent people were killed in cold blood by the Deep State in India which is still thriving.

Mr Ramadhar got a few of us to set up the Delhi chapter of the APDR, the Association for Protection of Democratic Rights. One of our illustrious members who continues to be active today in public life is Swami Agnivesh. We used to meet at Mr Ramadhar's house. At one meeting, Mr Ramadhar said, "let's go and meet all the political leaders". George Fernandes at this point had just been elected the leader of the Socialist Party of India, so one of the people we had to meet was him.

I was not a socialist at that point of time. I was far left from Lohia socialism and I continue to call myself a 'left socialist' and refuse to call myself a 'Lohia Socialist'. I think my readings on Socialism go far beyond the works of Dr Ram Manohar Lohia. I drank more deeply from the Marxian tradition outside the Communist parties epitomized by Acharya Narendra Deva. We went to see him for the release of the Naxalite prisoners. Immediately he said, "Yes. Happy to help." "I'll send out the leaflets to all the party units to join whatever local programmes you have. We must get these boys out."

I thought, "Wow. This guy is good!" Otherwise we got really stupid responses from most of the political leaders. We did the rounds and many of them looked at us as if we were people from Mars and that we had come to espouse a terrible cause. And here was a man who said, "yes, yes, send me everything that you want and I will try and do what I can do."

I got along closely with other socialists as well at the formative stage of my political thought process. There is a wonderful socialist, a retired professor of Hindi, Professor Rajkumar Jain. Observing him, I understood for the first time what a Lohia Socialist was. How the flame of Civil Disobedience had been kept alive. I could have easily thrown a Molotov Cocktail anytime. I had read how to manufacture them. Then, I saw the raw courage of this man, Rajkumar Jain who had been beaten to pulp by policemen numerous times and would still keep muttering the incantation, "*Hamla chahe jaisa hoga, haath hamara nahi uthega*". Meaning "irrespective of the violence perpetrated on me, my hand will not be raised in anger."

The radical left wing socialist in me realized that it took more courage to do that than throw something and scoot. I realized that Rajkumar Jain had more courage than all of us wannabe Che Guevaras with our berets.

It took more courage to stand there and get beaten to pulp and keep muttering this incantation, like a Buddhist chant. The man is incredible.

Paul Fernandes mentioned George being beaten in 1963 in Bombay at Dadar railway station. The police had every intention of killing him. They were raining *lathi* blows on his head in particular.

Mr Kannamwar was a terrible human being, then Chief Minister of Maharashtra. He was an early genetic clone of what we have today. Men of Straw as Chief Ministers.

I was told later by my socialist friends that somebody who they all thought was a socialist party worker from the local Gujarati community pulled out his revolver, pointed it at the Bombay police and said, "I am Special Branch", meaning, the Intelligence, stating that they could not kill George. That is how George was saved, otherwise they had beaten him 'black and blue' and he would have died.

Dayabhai Patel was the name of the officer who saved him. Of course, he was ousted; because he did this, he was no longer useful to the Intelligence on the Socialist Party. Long story, short, when George became Minister of Industries in 1977, there was a vacancy for the Chief Vigilance Officer in a public sector undertaking (PSU). Dayabhai had just retired from the Police in Ahmedabad. George asked me to find his number and he asked him, "Dayabhai, would you like to come to Delhi and be the Chief Vigilance Officer of a PSU in your post retirement stage?" and it was a good job that he did.

I am only trying to say that the Deep State never trusted George. He may have been part of the state machinery, but the Deep State is different from the state machinery. Please understand this, yesterday, today and tomorrow. And this is what many socialists and Indians don't understand. We point fingers at Pakistan, and the ISI, while we have something equivalent here. Except that we are not as crude as the Pakistanis are. The Deep State in India is therefore very much alive and kicking. I'll give you another example later.

When I got involved in the Socialist movement, I was only 19. He appointed me as the Joint National Convener of the Free Kista Gowd and Bhoomaiah Committee. They were two peasants who were politically Maoist who had killed a rapacious landlord. The Chairman was George and we ran this campaign. Unfortunately the Emergency came and both of them were hanged during it.

We had meetings in every state capital and many district headquarters. For the first time, it allowed George to draw several former boys and girls who were fascinated with the Naxalite movement like me, not ideologically committed but out of sheer anger about the situation that prevailed in India at that time. George brought them to his Trade Unions. A lot of them became trade unionists, others became political workers. Some like Bhabani

Shankar Hota became a Member of Parliament in 1977.

Immediately after the Janata government was formed under Morarji Desai in 1977, very few people knew that Mr Charan Singh, for whatever wonderful things he did for rural development, had no clue to internal security and the rule of law. Mr Singh was going to bring in the same law of Preventive Detention, the Maintenance of Internal Security Act (MISA) that had lapsed during the Emergency.

Fortunately we had a few good Socialists, Mr Madhu Limaye in Parliament and including George, four in the Cabinet. Madhu Limaye in Parliament had given a fiery speech stating that he would 'bring down' the government if the law was passed. George was able to convince Morarji Desai that this was a very bad idea. Morarji Desai had to then gingerly walk around Charan Singh. Mr Charan Singh was as prickly as a porcupine as to what he considered as his turf.

Charan Singh's draft on Preventive Detention became the National Security Act (NSA) when Indira Gandhi came back to power in 1980.

I created a problem for George while he was Minister. In 1978, the Shah of Iran was coming to India. I was close friends with Iranian students studying in India who were opposed to the Shah of Iran, whether they were Islamic or leftist. They all stayed in my house. I still remember Persian slogans, *MarghbarPahlevi*, the equivalent of 'Pahlavi Murdabad'. So I helped organize a demonstration. I helped all the Iranian students from Aligarh, Jalandhar, Pune, and Bangalore find accommodation and kept them in houses of friends including the house of the Indian High Commissioner in Mauritius at that point of time which was a comfortable three storeyed house. The police were looking at cheap hotels and guest houses. There were no mobiles, so on the day of the demonstration, I had a student on a motorcycle stand near the technical area of the airport and told him, "the minute you hear the commotion in the technical area, don't wait for the entourage. When you hear the commotion and the aircraft landing, scoot and come to Baba Kharak Singh Marg where all the emporiums are." Every Iranian, JNU or Delhi University student I could round up was inside the various emporiums busily handling silk that he or she could never buy. They were "shoppers".

The police themselves were our last signal system because we knew that they would close the barricades as soon as the entourage crossed Willingdon Crescent which is quite a distance away. So the minute the police blocked the traffic, I knew that they were coming in the next five minutes. So we lit out of the lobby of the Rivoli cinema and there's a wonderful photograph in the *Hindustan Times* of me jumping on the bonnet of the lead car. Of course the Shah was perturbed and the Government of India embarrassed. Earlier the ceremonial drive was taken through the inner circle of Connaught Place and then on to Rashtrapati Bhavan through Janpath. All ceremonial drives were stopped after that.

There was hell to pay when we were all arrested and taken to Parliament Street police station and the police found I was working with a Union Minister. So the phones buzzed, the Superintendent of Police of the New Delhi district came in sheer horror and said, "Mr Nair you must leave immediately!" So I said, "No, I'm not leaving, till all these boys and girls are leaving with me." Around two hours later I get a frantic call from Ashok Jaitly on the police station phone. Ashok was then George's special assistant from the IAS, saying that Morarji Desai's secretary had called saying that Mr Desai has ordered for everyone to be released.

The next morning, George didn't say a word. I thought I was going to lose my job and get fired but he just smiled and did not say a word. I was back at work and he said, "Get my appointments fixed!" So I went about, fixing his appointments. So that was his thing—that protests and dissent were fine. I don't think any other boss would have kept me a day longer especially when the Cabinet had to discuss what my friends and I had done.

The second incident I would like to talk about is when Father Anthony Murmu was killed. He had been a Member of Parliament from what is now Jharkhand. He was a Jesuit priest. But he was an unconventional priest, not wholly welcome in the official Catholic Church hierarchy, a Theology of Liberation Priest. He was a wonderful person. A tribal himself, he was a great fighter for tribal rights. He lost his seat in 1980 with Indira Gandhi's return but continued to work for tribal rights and fight against land acquisition by mining corporations in that area. Father Anthony was shot by the police and killed in 1985.

Every one forgot him. Only George remembered him. He went and made sure that a lifelong pension from the New India Cooperative Bank was given to his widow. This was a big thing for a small tribal family who had no real means of sustenance. And it was done without any publicity. I'm mentioning it for the first time publicly. The wife did not want the publicity. She always said that if the information was made public, all her relatives would jump on her and ask for a share.

The NSA was enacted in 1980, immediately after the second coming of Mrs Gandhi—she was a control freak. We got a tip off from a Junior official in the President's Secretariat that the draft Cabinet note for approval had gone to the President's Secretariat for his signature. George, of course, made hell in Parliament and the Press picked it up massively. The first arrest coincidentally was that of a well known socialist and trade unionist of the Gujarat Mazdoor Panchayat, P. Chidambaram, who was leading the Anti-Reliance agitation in Patalganga. This is where the big Rayon Factory set up by a carpet bagger, then darling of the Congress and now benefactor of the BJP, is situated.

Then A.K. Roy was arrested. A wonderful independent Marxist and Member of Parliament who came from what is today Jharkhand, then South Bihar. And NSA was used massively thereafter. Indira Gandhi had on numerous occasions in Parliament said that NSA would not be used against political workers and was meant only to be used against bootleggers and smugglers, and 'anti-social' elements.

This is a funny term intelligible in the context it is used, only in India—the word "anti-social"—some foggy bureaucrat in the Home Ministry must have conjured up this word.

In early 1982, late at night at 9 pm, George received a call from Mr K.G. Kannabiran, a famous lawyer, who before his death was the President of the People's Union for Civil Liberties—a wonderful person—saying that Kondapalli Seetharamaiah, an important Maoist leader, had been arrested at Hyderabad railway station and the police would take him to the jungles of Warangal—to shoot him, in a so-called 'encounter'. What we euphemistically call "encounter" is actually an extra-judicial execution.

The call came around 9 pm. I was not at Tughlaq Crescent where George lived. I had gone home earlier. Fortunately I had a phone at home. So George immediately called me and said "Get back Ravi, quick!" I had a motorbike that I rode like a madman and came back. He had already told me what had happened on the phone. He gave me a handwritten letter for Justice P.N. Bhagwati who was at that point a member on the bench in the Supreme Court.

Shortly after 10.30 pm, I woke up Justice Bhagwati at his house. He had only one security guard—not the platoon of guards we have today—I just brushed past him. Being the good, crazy socialist, I knew how to deal with officious cops. I told Justice Bhagwati that I had a letter from George and it involved a man's life and that he needed to act immediately. He said, "what can I do now?" I said, "you give me your handwritten order on your letterhead, sign your name to it, I will go to the telegraph office, send the telegrams immediately to the District Superintendent of Police, the District Judge, and Inspector General of Police and others and we'll see what happens. That's the best we can do". That saved his life. The telegrams got there on time and he was produced in Court instead of being killed in an encounter. Another age, another time.

This was George. He was willing and happy to work late at nights. He did not go to sleep till I came back and said, "I've sent the telegrams" to which he said, "all right, now call Kannabiran". There were not even STD phone calls at that time. So you had to book what was called a lightning trunk call and wait.

I finally got through and informed Mr Kannabiran about what had been done and he said, "you have done what you can and early in the morning I will see what can be done. The minute they produce him in court, I will make sure that nothing untoward happens".

Then came the Sri Lanka issue. In 1983, the first Tamil refugees came from Sri Lanka. Having studied in Madurai for two years, I speak colloquial Tamil. So George immediately put me in touch with the Tamils who came to see him and we were able to stop the deportation of Mr Chandrahasan through a court order and lobbying. He now heads a major refugee NGO, known to be close to the Indian Home Ministry.

We were also able to stop the deportation of a large number of other Tamil refugees many of whom now live in Canada, the United Kingdom and other European nations.

The Burmese and the Tibetans were causes that George had a special place for. In fact I met Lodi Gyari, who was the Dalai Lama's representative in North America as a young person. Lodi was then the General Secretary of the Tibetan Youth Congress (TYC). This was in 1977. He had gone on a hunger strike with the TYC outside the UN office in Lodhi Road. So George said "listen, he's not going to break the fast unless somebody big arrives". So we got Acharya Kripalani who had been the grandfather of the whole Janata Party government at that point.

The Foreign Ministry was against George getting involved. Jagat Mehta, then Foreign Secretary, I recall, called George saying, "Please don't do this! We're not to interfere in this". He was a good Foreign Secretary. Mr Vajpayee, then Foreign Minister of course, was too embarrassed to talk to George, knowing George, he knew that it was of little use. I was one of the underground couriers for George during the Emergency. One of the letters that I carried was to Atal Bihari Vajpayee when he was on parole. The letter pertained to whether the parties in opposition should participate in secret talks with Mrs Gandhi's emissaries about the future of the emergency. George was opposed to this.

Mr Vajpayee in his very poetic style in Hindi said, "George is willing to stay in jail and you people are willing to blow up things. I don't want to go back to jail. I'm happy to be on parole". So much for Atal Vajpayee. I was accompanied by Arun Kumar, then a UNI Correspondent very opposed to the emergency.

The next major challenge came with the Burmese issue and the Arakan issue—on which India is still floundering. India does not know whether it is in sixes or nines. Thanks to successive and including the present National Security Advisor who don't know much about the politics of the Arakan region of Myanmar.

The Arakan Liberation Army is the army of the Arakanese Buddhist community. They were earlier giving information to the Indians about the Chinese trawler movements in the Arakan Sea, the Bay of Bengal and the Andaman Sea.

The Chinese were spying on the Sriharikota missile base and the

Vishakhapatnam naval base. The Chinese trawlers were snooping. The Arakan Liberation Army was not given any material support but RAW had given them permission to transfer their arms bought in South East Asia to the Andaman Islands.

I wrote to George. I wasn't working with him then. In 1985, I had gone away to London and pursued Human Rights work as I didn't want to touch George's new friends in the right wing BJP. On my return in 1993, when he asked me if I wanted to join back, I told him frankly, "over my dead body. Not with the right wing". I was clear. But I had a strong loyalty and affection towards him as an individual especially having seen the courage that he operated with.

The Indian Tri Services in Operation Leech murdered the leadership of the Arakan Liberation Army; George ordered a CBI enquiry as Defence Minister on my writing to him. The military intelligence completely stymied the enquiry. A competent CBI officer, of the rank of Deputy Inspector General (DIG) from the Bihar cadre tried to investigate. None of the files of the military intelligence were opened to him. Later on, the government and RAW did a deal and all the boys were let out—the eleven who were not killed. The case was closed and they were allowed to leave the country.

George took up a case where forces under his overall command were involved in the killing of people, who were helping India. Today, the new Arakan armed opposition does not trust India and is closer to China.

Kashmir. I will not go into great details. Suffice to say that some of the contacts that George had with the Kashmiri underground were facilitated by me because I was one the first Indian civil liberties activists to go to Kashmir in 1991. The Indian Army and the CRPF were absent. The road from Boulevard Road to Lal *Chowk* was, as the Kashmiris said, 'liberated' area. You could not see any khaki or olive green uniform there. It was difficult to do civil liberties and work in that situation because the militants, the boys with the guns didn't want Indians, even the civil liberties activists there. They just said that they "don't want any Indians".

I differ with both Farooq Abdullah and Jaya Jaitly on the level of alienation. I think they are completely alienated. I would agree with Mr Chidambaram who in a moment of honesty said that "we are there in Kashmir only because the army is there".

I did not always agree with George. Gujarat 2002. George took out his Peace March in Ahmedabad; I called him and said "this isn't enough". I said "you have to publicly condemn Modi". Modi was then Chief Minister. I said "this man has allowed the thugs to run riot!" One of my informants was the recently retired Director General of Police, Mr Namboothri. Justice J.S. Verma who was then Chairman of the NHRC had asked him to see me.

I argued with George. We agreed to disagree. He said, "I've taken out the Peace March and got the message across". I replied, "but what about public condemnation of this thug?"

Our second major difference was when the Protestant Pastor, Mr Staines and his children were burnt alive in Odisha. He again made some, not so great remarks—to put it mildly. Obviously Vajpayee was using him as the Christian buffer. I did a critical report, which is on my website till today. Here I attacked the Justice Wadhwa Commission and I wrote a few paragraphs on George's pusillanimous role. I sent him a copy.

A few months later, Iftikhar Gilani, a Kashmiri and an excellent journalist married to the daughter of Syed Ali Shah Gilani, the leader of the Hurriyat, was arrested on a completely false case of "official secrets". The charge was that he had maps of military camps. Everything, which as a journalist, had been downloaded from the web, to mark out whenever he wrote a story to see which village was is in which district in the vicinity of a military camp.

He was then the Delhi Bureau Chief of the *Kashmir Times*. To George's credit, in his own ministry, he made enquiries, found that it was a completely cooked up case by the Intelligence Bureau.

He had the then Director-General of Military Intelligence (DGMI) Mr O.S. Lochab go to the magistrate's court to give evidence on behalf of the Defence Ministry, against the Home Ministry's concocted story, saying that there was nothing official and nothing secret about the seized material. The case was dropped.

The government was embarrassed. Mr Advani was embarrassed as they had to release him. Of Mr Advani, Mr Vajpayee is reported to have said, "my problem isn't my left knee or my right knee, its

Advani". (At that time, Mr Vajpayee required operations on both his knees.)

I can tell you many such stories—the Bhutanese refugees, the support he gave to Dan Gallin, in his efforts to isolate some Latin American governments on behalf of the International Union of Food Workers on the Latin American Food Workers Strike—including the Coca Cola strike in Columbia. When Lech Walesa was fighting the Communist dictatorship, George allowed me and my friends from JNU and Delhi University to do a yearlong picket; every Saturday from 2 in the afternoon to 6 pm in the evening, we hung around the Polish Embassy with big banners saying "Free Walesa" and the Poles were embarrassed. I got the idea from the permanent picket, back when I was living in London, outside the South African Embassy which the Anti-Apartheid movement did for many years. I said, "if they can do it why can't we?" We never had more than ten people, except on a few major occasions. George would make it a point to invite us all for a cup of tea if he was in town on a Saturday.

The "forgive and forget" thing. Professor Anand Kumar said George was very anti-Congress, which he was. It was very difficult to persuade him that politics had moved on. I had an argument with him on, of all days, his birthday.

I told him that the main threat was no longer Congress but right wing Hindu authoritarianism. We agreed to disagree. The "forgive and forget" thing crossed my mind when Anand said that George could never forget what happened to his family and friends like Snehalata Reddy and others who were badly tortured during the Emergency. After the Emergency, I was the hothead. I wanted to give a hiding to the three possible conduits that the intelligence had used to get to George. I had identified all three of them. I don't think anybody else knows them till today. So I said, "look, I will take them for a ride and give them a bashing". He gave me a blasting. I realized that this man was a genuine Christian. You know, one of those, "turn the other cheek". Anyway, I got a toasting and that was the end of the matter.

And horror of horrors, I shall not mention names because there are very distinguished people. I will write them in my autobiography. A very distinguished person shut the door on my face during the Emergency when I had gone to collect some money on George's instructions, for the Prisoners' Relief Fund. There were many party workers who were in prison and their wives and children were destitute so we had started a small fund. While we got some positive reactions, some were terrible. This man shut his door on my face in his Jor Bagh house, the minute I told him that I had a letter from George who was in jail. He almost had a heart attack. Later, George appointed him as a Chairman in a major government undertaking in his capacity as Industry Minister. I asked George why he did that and he sat me down and said "what do you know what kind of compulsions people have? He's a good man. He'll do a good job. So don't look at everything in 'black and white'. Look at the 'grey' too". So I thought, "Oh! This is a relic of his seminary training".

Laldenga was in exile first in Beijing and then he went to Germany where he got refugee status. While in Germany, the Indian government told him that he could come for talks to India on a safe conduct pass for a few months, and if the talks failed, he could go back to his asylum country. The talks failed. He had two months of his safe conduct pass. He was put up in an IB safe house in Mehrauli. Laldenga came to George in panic. It was the first time George met him. Mr Laldenga told George that he had contacted the German Embassy but they would not take him back. Mrs Indira Gandhi had spoken to Helmut Schmidt, (who was the then Chancellor of Germany) and there was no way the Germans would take him back. So George said "All right. Come back to me after 3-4 days". He then asked me to explore possibilities. I did so, and it didn't work. Finally, Laldenga got to London, but that is another story.

We finally decided that if he got arrested, we needed a lawyer. My immediate response was to think of Ashok Panda, now a Senior Advocate in the Supreme Court. A competent lawyer committed to civil liberties. I called Ashok but he was on holiday in Odisha. My second choice was Swaraj Kaushal which led to him eventually becoming the Governor of Mizoram, and his claim to fame that he brokered the deal. It was actually George who talked him into it. George told Laldenga that the geopolitical situation had changed. "Make your peace with Mrs Gandhi. Come back to India and you'll get some space under the banyan tree".

After the 1984 riots, I went to ask for his help in the Simranjeet Mann case. He was happy to help. Simranjeet Mann had been tortured badly. His fingernails pulled out by electrical pliers. Jagmohan Singh, one of his co-accused was a former lecturer in Khalsa College, in Mumbai. No one was even willing to go to the railway station and give him clothes when he was arrested. Fortunately I was in Bombay, along with Ashim Roy, for some trade union work. Ashim and I rushed to the station where of course the Punjabi brawny cops were not letting us give him his clothes. Even his family was frightened to give him clothes while he was arrested and was being taken into custody because they were so terrified of the Punjab cops. Of course, both Ashim and I were old campaigners. We brushed past the cops, gave the clothes and handed over the cops a mouthful. George approved later.

When Prakash Singh Badal was arrested, under the NSA, all his political colleagues in other parties disappeared. Only George went and met his family. Prakash Singh's wife later said that "nobody knocked on our door when we were friendless in Chandigarh. You (George) knocked on our door."

When Yasin Malik was tortured badly in Agra, I went to George and said, "listen, you can't permit torture. Keep him in detention. But not torture". And he, for whatever it was worth, told the Home Minister. So Yasin was brought to Delhi, from Agra where he had been beaten black and blue.

One thing that Farooq Abdullah did not mention. In 1977, George got the brilliant idea to make Sheikh Abdullah, the Vice President of India, He sounded Morarji. Morarjibhai was an intelligent man. He immediately caught on to the idea and understood the significance. He said who better than you to go and make the offer. So it was a family trip with Leila, little Sannu and me. And we went to Sheikh Abdullah's house and George spoke to him in our presence. George did not want the Press to get wind of anything, so it was as if we were on a family holiday to Kashmir. And to keep up the pretence, we went to Gulmarg. He didn't have the time and he said, "what the hell am I going to do in Gulmarg?" But the pretence had to be kept so we went there.

Sheikh Abdullah was a gracious man and he, of course, said 'no' but the idea was that he would take over from Sanjeeva Reddy as President of India at some point. It would have made a lot of difference in India. George was thinking out of the box, which Morarji Desai had taken to immediately.

Finally, Farooq mentioned the meetings with the underground —this as Railway and Kashmir Affairs Minister. Mr V.P. Singh—I am not an admirer of him—was a disingenuous and Janus faced man. He and the Deep State had Mr Jagmohan appointed as Governor to stymie the efforts of George. The story of Dr Ahad Guru, a medical doctor, a highly paid professional, was a Central Committee member of the JKLF, appointed to talk to the Government of India through George. Dr Guru was killed by Hizbul militants after the story that he was talking to GOI was leaked by Intelligence sources to a senior journalist. He continues to be their henchman.

I had organized the first meeting. I was still operating from the basement of George's place in Hauz Khas even though I had left George a long time ago. The Intelligence kept telling him "No, he can't use the Minister of Railway's personal house even if it is a basement". I used to issue reports those days of the Indian Army going berserk. The Deep State stymied the efforts at peace in Kashmir. Someday there should be a public enquiry into Intelligence shenanigans and they should be brought under strict Parliamentary control. In fact, my only criticism of our Tibetan friends is that sometimes they become too good friends with the Indian Deep State in their Anti-Chinese narrative.

I will end with saying that George Fernandes, with one or two exceptions when he had to pull his punches, because of the official position he held, was always willing to help every time. Whether it was a case for commutation of Death Penalty, or getting somebody out of prison much to the consternation of some of his Cabinet colleagues.

He was courageous. I was the Secretary of the Baroda Dynamite Defence Committee, Justice Tarkunde was the chairperson. At every court hearing he was able to put Indira Gandhi's dictatorship on the back foot. It needed brains and just a sense of raw courage. It was difficult. I could see even some of his party colleagues trying to make their own private deals with the Emergency regime. George was very clear. He would go to boot hill before he sat with "that lady".

I'll end with this. He was a brave man. I salute him and respect him for that.

True Friend of Tibet and Tibetan People

Kalon Karma Yeshi

George meant a great deal for Tibet and Tibetan people. It was lucky for me to attend his funeral and burial on 31st January and 1st February with Tibetan delegates to pay our last tribute to this great soul. George Sahab, we say George lak, was a true friend of His Holiness the Dalai Lama. Whenever there was a need, he was always there with Tibetans. When Tibet was occupied by China in 1959, when we came to India, it was this great country and people who gave shelter to us. I was born in exile and I'm now a father to three children and whatever I am now, all because of this great country and people like George Sahab.

George was always there whenever there was a Tibetan meet or processions in Delhi or elsewhere in the world. He was always there as a great speaker, a great supporter. I always remember 3 Krishna Menon Marg, when we go to the city of Delhi to meet Indian politicians, sometimes we get appointments and sometimes not. But 3 Krishna Menon Marg was always different where George Sahab stayed. It was always open to us, we could get an appointment anytime. When I used to be a leader of the Tibetan organization called Tibet Youth Congress, those days when I was a student in Chandigarh, I first heard George Sahab speaking in Delhi. Whenever we went to his residence, it was always open. Not only us. I remember, the Burmese students' movement, the Bhutanese refugees, his house was open to everybody. He even said, "Karma, you can open your Tibetan office in my residence", but we said, "we are in India, we have our office in Dharamshala, and we have to have cordial relations with all the political parties". He also applauded us; like that was he a great soul. I also remember, in 1998, there was a big hunger strike movement in Delhi. In those days George Sahab was the Defence Minister. Two days later, the army chief of China came to India. George said China is the number one enemy of India and then later the Pokhran test happened. Incidentally, Buddha Smiles was the code for the test. So this was under the leadership of late Atal Bihari Vajpayee, the then honourable Prime Minister, and George Sahab that time gave us huge inspiration. We (our people) were on a hunger strike for almost sixty plus days and there were many supporters who always used to raise concern about Tibetan people like "How you people are doing at Jantar Mantar?". George was there with us time and again. Today, I'm meeting my very old friend, Dr Sunilam from Madhya Pradesh after twenty plus years. We were together in many international conferences, to raise the issue of Tibet and he was also there to support us. Today, again because of George Sahab, I'm meeting him. So, like that there are many friends at this gathering. So once again, this great soul was a true socialist, a true friend of Tibet and Tibetan people. Even when his health was not good, he visited Dharamshala to grace the occasion of the 50th anniversary of the Tibetan National Uprising Day in Dharamshala. Like that he was there with us every time, every moment and anytime. I once again pay sincere tribute to George Sahab on behalf of Tibetan people in and outside Tibet.

George has left us but his wisdom, his thoughts will remain forever. Mahatma Gandhi died in 1948 but his thoughts, his beliefs, his thinking are still very much alive. Likewise, George Sahab's wisdom and thoughts will remain forever. I once again would like to mention that we have lost a great friend and supporter. As rightly said by His Holiness the Dalai Lama, we believe he will be reborn again and not only to raise the issues of people in this great country but also be a true supporter of Tibet once again. I want to thank George Sahab's family for standing behind us for so many years. We have really lost a great friend and we really need greater friends and supporters like him. Tibet right now is going through a critical juncture. I met George many times at his residence and still cannot believe he is not with us.

Tibet Salutes the Legacy of George Fernandes

Dolma Gyari

I consider myself fortunate to have had the privilege of knowing George Sahab from my early age and more so to have regular interactions with him I have beautiful memories in my heart. His departure has created a huge vacuum in the whole Indian democratic system. It is an end of an era on all accounts. A great loss for Tibet.

His Holiness, the Dalai Lama, at the sad demise of George Sahab said, "I have told him, at times when I met him, that I will always remember him". His Holiness speaks on behalf of and is the Voice of Tibet. I would humbly echo those words and say that I shall always remember George Sahab! He will always remain in my heart as a great human being, a great supporter of Tibet and a very dear revered family friend. Above all, one of the greatest leaders that the world has ever seen. The history of the Tibetan people's struggle for restoration of the freedom in Tibet, is incomplete without him.

I remember George Sahab say that his association with Tibet was since even before he first personally met with His Holiness. The great Indian Socialist leader Dr Ram Manohar Lohia, was vocal and active in expression of support of the Tibetan people. He spoke strongly against unjust forceful occupation of Tibet by the PRC, describing it as "Child Murder". Young George Sahab was highly inspired and felt in his heart the misery that the people of Tibet were suffering. Coming back to what I was trying to say about George Sahab's first fight for the Tibetan cause, I think it was in 1959. George Sahab telephoned the Chinese Consulate in Bombay and asked them to receive a Memorandum. But on arrival there, he and his delegation of about a thousand workers found the

Consulate gate closed but through the open windows, they could see people looking outside. Using a mike, he called them to receive the memorandum. And as we all know, once George Sahab decides upon something, nothing can stop him. He then got his worker to bring rotten tomatoes and eggs. He also got a volunteer to get a picture of Chairman Mao. Next, the rotten tomatoes and eggs were like darts, aimed at the picture. I remember him also mentioning with a twinkle in his eyes that later, Dr Ram Manohar Lohia told him that it was a stupid thing to do!

This incident annoyed the Chinese so much that they made formal protest to the Government of India. They asked for an unconditional apology from the government. Prime Minister Nehru immediately wrote back describing the democratic political system of India with many political parties and that they should not take it seriously. This letter went to Zhou Enlai and a reply came "We do not care about your political system. We demand an unconditional apology and we will neither forget nor forgive for a hundred years". Yes, this he described as his first association with the Tibetan issue and from that day, George Sahab has been, as he would say, on the side of His Holiness and the Tibetan people.

Yes, it is difficult to forget George Sahab. It is another matter that George Sahab in his major official responsibilities visited China and was well received. He was a true friend and upholder of Truth, Justice and Human Rights. His position was consistent and unchanged. While in the opposition, he would lead the Tibetan Freedom Movement in the streets of Delhi, organize international network of parliamentarians to help Tibet resolve the issue based on the Middle Path proposal of His Holiness. Similarly, while in the Government, he would not hesitate to describe China as potential enemy No.1. Yet again many years later, in an interview with Karan Thapar's Devil's Advocate programme, he said that China is still potential threat No.1 and could become enemy no 1. Friends or foe, that is George Sahab, fearless, outspoken, knowledgeable and witty—our beloved legendary leader, is a man that nobody can forget for hundred years to come. That is an aspect of the legacy that he leaves behind.

As for myself, whose fatherland is under foreign occupation, I've always looked up to George Sahab. I mean, since my very young age, I always remember having seen and known George Sahab. I don't remember, when was the first time that I actually met George Sahab. Fortunately for me, my brother Lodi Gyari Rinpoche, worked very closely with George Sahab. In fact, you could say George Sahab guided and supported Lodi in his service to His Holiness and the Tibetan cause. They were introduced to each other by none other than Shri Dr Ram Manohar Lohia ji. He asked George Sahab to help train Lodi. Over the decades their association blossomed into a very beautiful relationship, that lasted till the very end. Former special envoy of His Holiness, Lodi Gyari Rinpoche left for the heavenly abode on the 29th November and shortly after, on 29th January, former Chairman of NDA George Sahab has left us.

I am indeed blessed!! Fortunate to have personally met and known leaders of the stature of George Sahab. We remain greatly inspired by their selfless love for their nation and their sincere passion to work for a Free World. The story of India's Azadi continues to inspire many like me. I do wish for many George Sahabs and many like him to be born and raised among the Tibetan community. This I believed would definitely strengthen our movement. Thoughts like this often cross my mind. I salute them, their legacies continue to inspire us, even to this day, even if physically they are no longer with us.

During the visit of the Chinese Premier Li Peng to India, Tibetan people all around actively protested to express anguish and to draw attention to the critical situation inside Tibet. I was a new parliamentarian, and Karna Yeshe la was serving his first term in the central Executive of the Tibetan Youth Congress. The problem was that our request to hold protest demonstrations was not being entertained by the Delhi Police. The media carried more pictures of our peaceful resistance against the Delhi Police to remove us than the story of Tibet and China's misrule. The venues of these protest demonstrations were mainly outside the Chinese Embassy or the Boat Club, India Gate. Volunteers had poured in to Delhi from different parts of India but we were doing not much, except getting arrested. It was sad and very frustrating. Tibetans inside Tibet did not have the freedom to express their feelings nor protest. Tibet is under virtual Martial law. And those of us, in free

India, were not able to represent them properly. We needed to raise voice for them, on their behalf. We poured our heart out to George Sahab. He asked Jayaji to make a few calls and got some papers prepared. And that resulted in the suo moto order of the Court that even Tibetan refugees are entitled to the basic Fundamental Rights enshrined in the Constitution of India. This helped pave way for an organized, lawful and effective protest demonstrations. A few decades later, in an interview to *The Tibet Post*, George Sahab said, "these refugees have human rights in India. Shouting, demonstrating, and protesting are within their rights. Never should a Tibetan be arrested in India for exercising his personal freedom."

This was a great breakthrough. I think after that the police first identified Parliament Street and later Jantar Mantar, as the designated place to assemble for protest demonstrations. The Tibetan protesters are treated on par with the citizens of India. This could not have happened without the timely joint efforts of George Sahab and Jayaji.

Dr Lobsang Sangay, President of the Central Tibetan Administration, described him as the strongest voice for Tibet. That therefore, the Tibetan community, people who are denied human rights, people struggling for democracy have lost our strongest voice. It is true for not only the Tibetans, his heart and home was open for all.

We shall always miss George Sahab. He is irreplaceable and leaves a huge vacuum that may never be filled. I have always loved him for what he was, and for the values that he stood for. I am so fortunate to have met him, to have learnt from him, to have had the good fortune on a few occasions to travel with him outside and inside the country. I do hope that we will, in our own small ways, be able to carry forward his legacy.

Champion of Civil Rights

Gurulingappa M. Patil

I represent Jagadguru Sri Shivarathreeshwara Mahavidya-peetha, Mysore, headed by His Holiness Jagadguru Sri Sri Shivarathree Deshikendra Mahaswamiji with whom George Fernandes Sahab had a very close association for more than four decades.

To me, George Sahab was the colossal personality and social leader this country has ever produced. "One should learn from the past but one should not live in the past. My concern is to look to the future, learn from the past, and deal with the present". These are the golden words of one of the heroes of Indian politics, George Fernandes, for whom politics was the way of pursuing ideas, principles and convictions, even though the path was strewn with thorns. For those familiar with Indian politics, from the 1960s till the first half of the last decade, his name was synonymous with struggle and an indomitable fighting spirit, experiencing the life of Bombay's footpaths and the plight of working people. He dreamed of a world free of poverty, injustice, and exploitation. He was frank and fearless, forthright and far-sighted; he made a valuable contribution to our country. He was among the most effective voices for the rise of the poor and marginalized and was a practitioner of the liberation of theology. Born into a Catholic family in Mangalore in Karnataka State, a proud son of the State of Karnataka in this country on June 3, 1930, his parents named him after King George V as the monarch was also born on the same day. His family intended to make him a Catholic priest but he left the place at the age of 18 for Bombay, the megacity of socialist India, looking for a job. In his twenties, George Fernandes started organizing industrial workers. Like many of his generation, he was also inspired by Sri Ram Manohar Lohia. He organized many labour strikes and agitations in the 1950s and 60s. George Sahab's surprising victory from South Mumbai against the S.K. Patil of the Congress in 1967 marked his entry in politics earning him the tag, Giant Killer. My heartfelt tribute to this veteran and socialist leader who never deviated from his ideology. He along with like-minded leaders opposed the state of Emergency from 1975 to 1977, for a period of 21 months. This resulted in the defeat of the government led by Prime Minister Indira Gandhi. He became the Union Minister of Industries in the coalition named the Janata Party. A visionary Railway Minster and a great Defence Minister, who made India safe and strong. He was the Defence Minster of the Indian government when India fought the Kargil War in 1999. It was in his tenure that India conducted nuclear tests in Pokhran in 1998. He resisted the Emergency tooth and nail. His simplicity and humility were noteworthy. Referring to his stint as Defence Minister, Sri Venkaiah Naidu said that he also paid a record number of 32 visits to the world's highest battlefield at Siachen Glacier to boost the morale of the nation's personnel working in arduous conditions. At the age of 73 in June 2003, he wore a flying suit and took off in a SU 30 Fighter Jet plane from Lohegaon Airport station near Pune. He had a strong bonding and association with His Holiness Jagadguru Sri Sri Shivarathree Deshikendra Mahaswamiji and as a result of which, irrespective of protocol, he visited his Technical Education Campus—JSS Academy of Technical Education, Noida campus where I am presently heading as Principal—without informing his protocol officers and local administration of Noida, in order to seek the blessings of His Holiness Mahaswamiji.

All were puzzled, his security guards, the Protocol officials, including the district administration of Noida and they made frantic efforts to locate the Defence Minister who was at the JSS Academy of Technical Education, Noida. Then the security started hovering around the entire campus.

Again on August 1, 2003, he presided as Guest of Honour in JSS Academy of Technical Education, Noida, where the former President of India, the late Dr A.P.J. Abdul Kalam, dedicated the Jagadguru Sri Shivarathreeshwara Mahavidyapeetha, JSS Academy of Technical Education, Noida to the nation.

I recall his slogan, "jab tak bhooka insaan rahega, tab tak

dharti par toofan rahega." He was a champion of civil rights and struggled for the poor, the weak, the downtrodden and the underprivileged farmers. It is therefore that the Indian youth today appreciates the extraordinary grit and courage of the man called George Fernandes. Those who wish to learn from the twists and turns of independent India's history, and are committed to build a better India can't ignore him or the times that shaped him.

He may have physically left us, but his ideas and values live on in all of us in this country. And he is an example of one who made us—everybody in the country and the world— realize that mountains can be moved with patience and determination.

George Fernandes: A Humble Giant

George Mathew

While recalling the life of George Fernandes, my thoughts go back to the 1970s, 1980s and up to the mid-90s. That was the period when contemporary political issues were linked with very harsh and intense realities of his life. Over these three decades, he was in the thick of the working class movement, social and political struggles, challenging the prevailing corrupt, oppressive and dehumanized systems of governance with his reckless courage. In his fight for the poor and the oppressed, he spoke and wrote with a fervour and realism unmatched in contemporary times. Known as a militant socialist, George was too impatient to stick to a political party. He was a leader who redefined the labour movement in India as an effective weapon of political struggle; a revolutionary who took to underground resistance in fighting the Emergency of 1975-77; a giant-killer and sometimes, a fighting loser at the hustings. He was a natural socialist and trade unionist, an unfailing friend of the working class, a human rights activist with an international perspective, and a unique politician who dared to be in the eye of almost every storm.

How George fought against multinational corporations and capitalists in order to address the concerns of the teeming millions of India is history. He advocated employing new methods of harnessing science and technology without snapping the harmonious bond between man and nature in economic and development strategies.

Apart from his unflinching faith in the efficacy of democratic socialism for resolving India's socio-economic problems and ameliorating the status of the poor and the dispossessed, George, over the years, developed a deep interest in the growth of international socialism as well. He enriched it by giving it a new dimension and orientation keeping in view the needs of the people in the Third World. He did not fight shy of taking up cudgels against his European counterparts whenever he felt that their approach was sectarian and did not encompass the hopes and aspirations of people in the developing and underdeveloped countries.

George Fernandes made history of sorts by being in and out of prison no less than fifty times in post-Independence India, for periods ranging from a week to a year. During most of these incarcerations, he was denied such common amenities as books and periodicals and was, more often than not, treated as a 'C' class prisoner. The deprivation of writing facilities in jail engendered a unique elocutionary style in George's speeches and writings.

The path of history George trod as a noble leader in independent India is embodied in the three volumes published as his 60th birthday *festschrift* by the Institute of Social Sciences. Since the mid-70s, when I was in Jawaharlal Nehru University doing my PhD, George Fernandes was my inspirational guru.

At a meeting in New Delhi with Dr Johan Galtung, who was then Professor of Peace Studies in the University of Hawaii and an admirer of George, I had discussed with him the idea of bringing out a volume of essays by eminent persons on the theory and practice of socialism and democracy to felicitate George on his 60th birthday. Encouraging this effort, he suggested the title: 'Dignity for All'—George's life having been an unflinching struggle for this paramount cause. However, when I mentioned to George that some of us were planning this *festschrift,* he politely refused to have any celebration on his 60th birthday. I did not heed his words in this case and went ahead.

During a subsequent discussion I had with Professor U.R. Anantha Murthy, then Vice-Chancellor of the Mahatma Gandhi University (Kerala), a comrade-in-arms of George, he was of the view that many of George's writings and speeches were of historical value and that they should be published along with 'Dignity for All'. When I began working on it, I realized the enormity of the task. George had no systematic collection of his writings or clippings or notes of his speeches. However, a number of his friends enthusiastically came forward to help and that resulted in the mega volume: *George Fernandes Speaks,* a selection of his speeches and writings of 25 years (1965-90).

Meanwhile, during a meeting I had with Madhu Limaye, the veteran socialist leader, I requested him to contribute an essay to Dignity for All. He readily agreed and began to write on a hitherto unresearched subject: 'Socialist Communist Interaction in India', and delightfully, the *festschrift* blossomed into a full-fledged book. Thus, in George's 60th birthday year, three volumes of lasting value—1. *George Fernandes Speaks,* 2. *Dignity for All,* and 3. *Socialist Communist Interaction in India*—were published. It was a great day in my life when V.P. Singh, former Prime Minster of India, released these three volumes under the general title Dignity for All in George's honour on April 12, 1991 at a special function in the Constitution Club, New Delhi, in the presence of S.R. Bommai, Rabi Ray, and many other national leaders of that time.

On the occasion of the Silver Jubilee celebrations of the Institute of Social Sciences in 2010 when we were pondering over the idea of organizing a special event to remember the valuable contribution of George to the Institute, we met an outstanding Burmese artist, Sitt Nyein Aye, who agreed to draw a portrait of George. He did it with special emotional attachment to George. As is well known, George's official residence at 3 Krishna Menon Marg, since 1989, was the home of young Burmese refugees for years, along with Tibetans and others. The Institute considered it a great privilege and honour that the portrait of the most powerful and dynamic, and, yet at the same time, most humble leader of the working class whom independent India has seen, was unveiled by His Holiness the Dalai Lama on November 19, 2010. His Holiness gave, on this occasion, an inspiring lecture on "Human Approach to World Peace". An excerpt reads:

> ... What is a human being? A human being is also a kind of social animal—there are many different species of social animals and we are one of them. But one unique thing about the human being is human intelligence that has progressed greatly, and, I think, it has also mobilized and organized violence.... In the 20th century, according to historians, through violence and wars, the number of people killed was over 200 million.... When we face some problems or disagree on something, we must meet our adversaries as friends, listen to them,

> share our views with them and make compromises. This is a human approach, wherever some disagreements exist. The ultimate goal should be to demilitarize the world because huge money is spent for these weapons, including nuclear weapons.

The Institute's family was especially happy that on this occasion, the Chairman of the Institute of Social Sciences Prof. U.R. Ananthamurthy, George's brothers: Michael, Paul and Aloysius, as well as two of his long-time close associates: Ravi Nair and Frederick D'sa were also present.

While George Fernandes's health was deteriorating with Alzheimer's disease, an idea came up to organize an international conference to remember his legacy. Thus, the Institute of Social Sciences, in collaboration with Asia Democracy Network and World Movement for Democracy organized such a conference on the theme: "Strengthening Democracy in Asia: Inclusion, Participation and Rights" in New Delhi on March 23-24, 2015. It got extraordinary support worldwide from his followers, friends and admirers from India and twenty other countries. For me personally, I was keen that George's long-time friend, His Holiness the Dalai Lama, should grace this occasion as the chief guest. Our friend, Tempa Tsering, Delhi representative of the Dalai Lama's Office, conveyed our invitation to His Holiness and he readily accepted it.

His Holiness, in his inaugural address, remembered the life and work of George Fernandes with fond memories. An excerpt:

> This is a special gathering. I appreciate how each one of you is committed not only to your own well-being, but to taking care of others. On this special occasion, we remember my old friend George Fernandes, who even after becoming the Defence Minister continued to maintain a simple, austere way of life based on self-reliance. Some of our friends' attitudes change once they come to exercise power; but not George's. He was sympathetic to Tibet and the Tibetan cause right from the start and never missed an opportunity to speak up for them. His face will remain in my heart till I die … and I'll remember him even in my next life!"

His Holiness was all praise for the secularism embodied in the Indian Constitution, saying it has brought "good results" in India. He said India has a rule of law and its democracy is deep rooted. "Barring a few exceptions, this country is most stable compared to others." Underlining the importance of freedom, His Holiness said "freedom is essential for human beings as it promotes creativity. This is true not only for human beings, even animals love freedom."

The Dalai Lama also advocated people-to-people contacts between India and Pakistan, saying, "it is very important. It must continue". According to His Holiness, India should welcome more Chinese students and Buddhist pilgrims to the country. Taking note of "some disturbances on account of political or military leaders for their narrow interests and propaganda", the Tibetan spiritual leader said "people should continue to have close relationships and that is the way to build trust." "In the struggle between the power of the gun and the power of truth, the power of the gun may be stronger in the short term, but in the long term it is the power of truth that prevails."

Carl Gershman, a friend of George for many years, came from the USA along with the US trade union leader Fred Redmond. The international scholars who spoke on the occasion include: Richard Gupwell, Chairman of the European Institute for Asian Studies in Brussels; Lobsang Sangay, Sikyong, Central Tibetan Administration, Tibet; Anselmo Lee, Co-Convener, Asia Democracy Network, Korea; Melinda Quintos de Jesus, former Steering Committee Member, World Movement for Democracy, Philippines; Shari Bryan, Vice President, National Democratic Institute, USA; Javed Ahmed Chandio, Executive Director, Center for Peace and Civil Society, Pakistan; Henri Tiphange, former Steering Committee Member, Asia Democracy Network, South Asia; Han Dongfang, former Steering Committee Member, World Movement for Democracy; Tom Garrett, Vice President, International Republican Institute, USA; Shahed Kayes, Cultural and Rights Activist, Bangladesh; Shawna Bader-Blau, Executive Director, Solidarity Center, USA; Marc Schleifer, Regional Director, Eurasia and South Asia, USA, and Selima Ahmed, President of the Bangladesh Women's Chamber of Commerce and Industry, Dhaka.

Also present on the occasion were Rita Bhandary, President of Federation of Women Entrepreneurs Association, Nepal; Corinna Lope, Regional Coordinator, South East Asian Committee for Advocacy, Philippines; Sherine Xavier, Executive Director, Home for Human Rights, Sri Lanka; Reena Khatoon, Programme

Manager for YP Foundation, New Delhi, and several other. Carl Gershman's idea was that this occasion must be woven around the legacy of George Fernandes to strengthen democracy in Asia through participation, inclusion and the upholding of universal human rights.

My thoughts go back to November 1984. During the anti-Sikh riots George took the lead in constituting the People's Relief Committee with Justice Hidayatullah as Chairman. By November 6, there were more than 60, 000 refugees in various camps in Delhi alone. As a member of the People's Relief Committee, I was also a member of the fact-finding committee along with S.K. Goyal, Sudhindra Bhadoria, Javed Habib and Yashwant Sinha. After struggling for more than six months the idea of establishing an institution in Delhi where intellectuals and activists could study contemporary social, political and economic issues and problems came up. A concept note was prepared for establishing an institution where researchers and activists could meet and through George's wholehearted support we have today the Institute of Social Sciences. He brought the basic starting fund from the trade unions of Bombay which enabled us to rent an office space in Safdarjung Enclave in New Delhi. There the foundation of the Institute of Social Sciences (ISS) was laid and George remained till his end a friend, philosopher and guide of the Institute.

In order to take forward the legacy of George Fernandes and to remember his great service to the people of this country the Institute of Social Sciences has taken the initiative to establish a Chair in his name, called the 'George Fernandes Chair on Labouring and Marginalized Peoples' at the Institute of Social Sciences.

This Chair will bring to national and international attention, the problems of the working class, the downtrodden and marginalized groups in our societies. We hope it will keep alive vibrantly the vision and mission of George Fernandes, the humble giant of India, for generations to come. Let me conclude with a quote from the introduction by eminent scholar and writer Professor Rajni Kothari to the book *George Fernandes Speaks* (1991):

> But what he [George Fernandes] has stood for and said and written is eminently worthy of our serious attention. Hence my readiness to do something I have never done before (despite having written so

many Forewords to academic books): write an Introduction to a book based on the output of a major politician of our country. One reason for accepting this assignment was my long-standing belief in the close inter-relationship between intellectual articulation and political action—and I see George Fernandes to be engaged in both, although he would himself, perhaps, like to play down the intellectual part, given his ambivalence to "armchair" intellectuals in a society crying out for major interventions on the practical plane. And yet, reading through the pages that follow, one is struck by the analytical brilliance of the author; these could well have been written by an academic with a radical democratic bent of mind although, to be frank, there aren't many such academics around.

Contributors

Anand Kumar, Professor of Sociology (Retd.), Jawaharlal Nehru University

Ash Narain Roy, Director, Institute of Social Sciences

Dick Gupwell, Political Advisor, Socialist Group, European Parliament (1976-1996); Chairman, *Jeevika Trust* (London) and European Institute of Asian Studies (Brussels)

Dolma Gyari, Former Deputy Speaker, Tibetan Parliament in Exile and former Home Minister, Central Tibetan Administration

Farooq Abdullah, Former Chief Minister of Jammu and Kashmir

Gurulingappa M. Patil, Principal, JSS Academy of Technical Education

George Mathew, Chairman, Institute of Social Sciences

Jaya Jaitly, President, Dastkari Haat Samiti and Former President, Samata Party

K.C. Tyagi, Member of Parliament, Rajya Sabha

Kalon Karma Yeshi, Finance Minister, Central Tibetan Administration

Michael Fernandes, President, Hind Mazdoor Kisan Panchayat

Neerja Chowdhury, Senior journalist and Political Commentator

Paul Fernandes, Political Leader and Social Activist, Toronto, Canada

Ravi Nair, Executive Director of the South Asia Human Rights Documentation Centre

Sumit Chakravartty, Senior Journalist and Editor, *Mainstream*

Suresh Prabhu, Union Minister, Commerce, Industry and Civil Aviation